TIGER'S TRIUMPH

TIGER'S TRIUMPH
Celebrating Sam Selvon

edited by

Susheila Nasta and Anna Rutherford

Dangaroo Press

Acknowledgements

The editors would like to thank Eve Williams, for permission to use 'The Keeper of the Temple' and *The Independent* for permission to reprint the photograph of Sam Selvon by Philip Meech. Thanks are also due to all contributors and publishers who agreed permission to reprint articles. Roydon Salick, 'Selvon and the Limits of Heroism: A Reading of *The Plains of Caroni*', first appeared in *Shades of Empire in Colonial and Post-Colonial Literatures* ed. C.C. Barfoot, Theo D'haen, (Rodopi, 1993); 'Sam Selvon: Interview with Reed Dasenbrock and Feroza Jussawalla' was taken from *Interviews with Writers of the Post-Colonial World*, eds. Dasenbrock, Jussawalla (University Press of Mississippi, 1992); Susheila Nasta, 'Setting Up Home In a City of Words: Sam Selvon's London Novels' is due to appear in *Other Britain, Other British. Essays in Contemporary Multi-Cultural Fiction*, ed. A Robert Lee (London: Pluto, due November 1995); Sam Selvon, 'Finding West Indian Identity in London' first appeared in *Displaced Persons*, eds. Kirsten Holst Petersen, Anna Rutherford (Dangaroo Press, 1988). Finally, and above all, the editors wish to thank the executors of Sam Selvon's literary estate.

Cover: 'The Keeper of the Temple' by Aubrey Williams

First published by *Kunapipi* in 1995
This edition first published by Dangaroo Press 1995

Australia   :   PO Box 1176, Armidale, NSW 2350
U.K.   :   PO Box 20, Hebden Bridge, West Yorkshire, HX7 5UZ

ISBN 1-871049 - 23 - 7

Printed in Great Britain by Villiers Publications, London N3.

CONTENTS

Sam Selvon by Philip Meech.

Sam Selvon

1923 - 1994

Foreword

When I come back here to Trinidad, I hear the kiskidee in the morning. You can identify yourself with the soil and the feeling of those sounds, and you instantly become part of the land.

Sam Selvon

... you took the small
language used by the island
for picong and calypsoes
and stretched its vowels
across the mouth of the world

Cecil Gray

Tiger's Triumph is a celebration of the life and work of the internationally distinguished Trinidadian writer, Sam Selvon, who died at the age of seventy one in April 1994. Sam, as many of the pieces in this collection will testify, was distinguished not only by the sheer range and variety of his published works - which include ten novels, numerous short stories, radio scripts, a screenplay as well as many other non-fictional essays collected together in *Foreday Morning: Selected Prose (1946-86)* [1] - but also by his influential position as one of the founding fathers of the Caribbean literary renaissance of the 1950s. Many ballads and eulogies were sung all over the world following Selvon's sudden illness and death during a brief trip home to Trinidad last year but one message seems to shine through all of these tributes and that is Sam's extraordinary warmth and generosity as a man, the depth of his vision as a natural philosopher, a writer to use a phrase from Ken Ramchand's memorial speech who was 'a believer fighting off unbelief' and his passionate attachment, despite the many years he spent abroad, to the land, to Trinidad. As he said in 1979, 'This island is my shadow and I carry it with me wherever I go.'

Most readers familiar with Selvon's work remember him primarily for his humour, his comic vision and his creation of easily accessible, picaresque and calypsonian characters whom one meets both on the streets of London and Port of Spain. He is also remembered importantly for his use of a creolized and non-Standard form of English both in his 'peasant' novels set in Trinidad - *A Brighter Sun* (1952) and *Turn Again Tiger* (1958) in which he gave voice and status to the East Indian cane community and heroic dimensions to his early character, Tiger - as well as in his famous London novels, *The Lonely Londoners* (1956), *Moses Ascending* (1975) and *Moses Migrating* (1983), where he colonizes England in reverse and liberates his black characters from standard

English and the entrapping stereotypes that surrounded them. Whilst there is a surface humour in all of these books, it is also important to note a far more serious side to Selvon's writing which is often disguised as simple naturalistic reflection and masks the profound sensitivity he felt about all the big questions in life, a sensitivity that is explicitly apparent in many of his non-fictional essays. As he wrote of the 'boys' in *The Lonely Londoners:* 'They only laughing because they fraid to cry'.

Selvon's range of literary talents was far larger than most people ever knew. Apart from the novels and short stories, there were reviews, essays, poems which he contributed to literary journals all over the world. Whilst he was in Britain between 1950-1978, many of his radio plays were broadcast. He was co-author for the first black feature film to be released in Britain, *Pressure* (1978). There were, later in life, other honours and awards, lectures and reading.

Sam was born in South Trinidad in 1923 and grew up in the small semi-rural town of San Fernando. He was the son of a dry goods merchant, a first generation East Indian immigrant to Trinidad, and an Anglo-Scottish mother. From an early age Selvon loved to write and listen to stories though he did not continue his formal education beyond High School. Always describing himself as a 'self-educated' man, Selvon was committed to becoming 'creolized', and to being a positive part of the cultural and racial mix of modern Trinidad. It was this pride in the hybridity of his background and his need as an artist to translate this vision into fiction, which resulted in his influential first novel *A Brighter Sun*. And it was this novel that established Selvon according to George Lamming as 'the greatest and therefore the most important folk poet the British Caribbean has ever produced'. Whilst this was an early statement of applause by Lamming (who travelled to England from the Caribbean on the same boat in 1950), and set up what is perhaps now in retrospect an unnecessarily extreme polemical opposition between Selvon's work and that of his fellow Trinidadian, V. S. Naipaul, it nevertheless pointed to a significant difference in the commitment of the two writers. For Naipaul, Trinidad could never be made in to anything; for Selvon, the celebration of the island was paramount even when as the title of one of his short stories suggests cane is bitter.

Selvon was never bitter or jealous of the success of others. In fact in 1990 he supported Naipaul's entry for an international literary award. He accepted his difference and was not interested in Naipaul's more glittering success; in fact he often joked about their different perspectives on race and the significance of 'home' by saying that old leopards can't change their spots. Sam never felt he had to try to impress; writing had always come first. Reputation was a bonus and he made no attempt at any stage in his career to falsely adapt his subject-matter to current trends or outside expectations of what 'black writing' should or should not be. In fact part of his decision to leave Britain for Calgary in the late

1970's was to do with this sense of beginning to be told what to write, whether it was Black Power politics or issues of gender. Selvon's art and his life have always formed 'a seamless whole'; he felt deeply about many of the political concerns of the day but refused to write propaganda, to destroy the integrity of his fiction by self-consciously espousing particular issues. As he said just after he left Britain in 1978: 'We have now to start thinking in terms of world literature, of contributing universally rather than ...merely with protestation novels, with days of slavery, with hardships of the black man...We want to rise above that'.

The pieces in *Tiger's Triumph* have been organised to reflect the many dimensions of both the man and his work. Creative pieces have been placed alongside the personal and the critical in a way which I hope reflects Sam's own feelings about the important need to cross over boundaries and mediate between a number of different voices and discourses. As will be obvious, the cover for this book depicts a leopard, in this case a mythical Mayan figure represented in a painting by the late Guyanese artist, Aubrey Williams. Whilst we know that you don't get leopards or 'tigers' for that matter in Trinidad, Sam has not only created an important 'Tiger' in Trinidadian literary history and the imaginations of many many readers - a 'tiger' like his character of that name who is rooted to the soil, to the mango tree and the kiskidee - but was also a special kind of Tiger himself, a tiger whose voice has risen from the language of the island and triumphed in stretching that language across the mouth of the world. This book celebrates Sam Selvon's achievement.

Susheila Nasta, 1995

NOTES

1. A full bibliography of Sam Selvon's fictional and non-fictional work is provided at the end of this collection which is edited by Ken Ramchand and Susheila Nasta (Longman, 1989, rpt. 1992) pp 226-248.

Main Books by Sam Selvon
   A Brighter Sun (1952)
   An Island is a World (1955)
   The Lonely Londoners (1956)
   Ways of Sunlight (1957)
   Turn Again Tiger (1958)
   I Hear Thunder (1963)
   The Housing Lark (1965)
   The Plains of Caroni (1970)
   Those Who Eat the Cascadura (1972)
   Moses Ascending (1975)
   Moses Migrating (1983)
   El Dorado West One (1988)
   Foreday Morning (1989)
   Highway in the Sun (1992)

ISMITH KHAN

Remembering Sammy

The title of one of Sam Selvon's novels is *Those Who Eat The Cascadura*. The cascadura is a small ancient, reptilian looking fish which lives in swamps. It is considered to be a delicacy, and especially so when fixed as a curry. Legend or myth has it that if you eat the cascadura you will return to end your days in Trinidad. Did Sam believe in that myth? Do we sometimes foresee the future? Or, does wishing it make it come to pass?

He died in Trinidad, was cremated, and his ashes buried there. It could have happened in England or Canada, but it did not. He rests besides members of his family in his hometown of San Fernando, and he was given a hero's funeral with all the pomp and ceremony that Trinidad could offer its native son. Once a 'Trini' always a 'Trini'. I am glad Sam returned to Trinidad, it would have been too lonely to be buried in England or Canada, both of which are far too cold for someone who loved the sun, loved his island, and loved his people. There is no longer a question of whether or not there is truth to the myth. He ate the cascadura, and he returned to Trinidad to end his days.

The first thought that crosses one's mind when a close friend dies - a friend who is one's own age - is one's own mortality. True or false? False - I think. His death has not led me to think of my mortality. Instead, I think of the days, the times we spent together. We met when we were sixteen and seventeen, and we met because his brother Dennis married my sister Betty. We have one nephew in common, we are writers, we both worked for the *Trinidad Guardian*, I as a reporter, Sam, as an inside man, he put together the Sunday section for the paper. He went to England, I came to the US at about the same time - around 1950.

Although he lived in London, and I in NYC or Michigan or California, we not only kept in touch by mail, but spent time with each other at the various literary conferences we attended: Trinidad, Guyana, Montreal, Toronto - and there were times when I visited with him, and he with me. We spent time in Scotland where he was a writer in residence. He arranged a lecture there for me, filled with colorful slides. That was before the day and age of video-cams. Later on I arranged for him to re-place me for one semester at the University of California in San Diego, and he lived with us for fourteen weeks. The Atlantic Ocean stood between us, but our friendship continued. No matter how much time passed between visits, whenever we met it was merely a question of picking up where our correspondence left off. And now there is only

silence, thoughts and remembrances, not mortality. That, I think comes
from the power of language, words, or perhaps homilies, and it is
alarming how they can shape our thoughts, forcing them into moulds
not of our making, because instead of mortality, I feel more alone than I
have ever felt in my life.

There were times when I thought as he did; that we thought and felt
the same things, reacted to people, friend or foe with the same kind of
reactions, and to have someone like that depart leaves a great void in a
world that is peopled by few. Our sense of alienation, no doubt because
of our background; living abroad was always there. Now it has grown
and escalated. Now the expression that one is always alone is far more
meaningful than it ever was - and what a terrible feeling that is - to see
and feel the full meaning of being alone in the world. So it is not
mortality, but the sense of alienation and aloneness that I wrestle with as
I think of his death at the age of seventy.

This is not a discussion of his work, literary critics have done that. Nor
is it a discussion of our domestic lives, and so I title it 'Remembering
Sammy'.

We talked about the past, growing up, and the things we did during
our 'boy-days' and I feel that a large part of our visits were in some ways
re-living, or re-capturing our days of growing up in Trinidad - running
away from school and going down to the sea, exploring un-frequented
parts of the island, going to Maracas Bay before a road was built - which
meant bicycling six miles to the foot-hills of Santa Cru where we left our
bicycles in the care of a watchman, hiked three miles up the mountain,
then three down with our back-packs filed with canned foods, mosquito
repellent etc. This trip was usually made over a long three day weekend.
We had to arrive early enough to cut down coconut branches to build a
tent for the night. We had to fetch fresh water from a stream, build a fire-
place (three or four boulders) to cook our meals as we listened to the
waves pound and roar, dash and tear at the beach till morning when we
got up with the sun and made our way down to the inlet where the
fishermen came in with their catch of snapper, Grouper, Kingfish and
sometimes lobsters.

The joys we knew, the pleasures we enjoyed were more than just
attempting to re-capture our 'boy-days'. It's as though we sensed that the
place we came from was no longer the same place - a place that we
thought we could always run back to if the winters got to be too cold, or
there was not enough money to pay the rent, or heat our rooms or
apartments. But that place was no longer there, and it was in our hearts
and our minds that we carried the beauty, the tranquility of a homeland
that was no longer what we had known. Perhaps we have been able to
re-capture that past for future generations as well as for ourselves to take
us through the sometimes joyful, sometimes painful life of the exile,
yearning for a past that no longer existed except in our hearts. And that

past did not include the nature of politics or history, it extended to things that were more basic, things like food and cooking, things like making and flying kites and catching those small flat fish called 'moonshine' with safety pins for hooks. Like most people who migrate we carried with us as our ancestors did, recipes, spices and herbs and the various ways we attempted to re-create dishes and flavors we grew up on. I recall him telling about letters he had received from his readers, not merely fan letters, but requests for recipes that his readers salivated over and wished to duplicate.

There is nothing that Caribbean people value more than dispensing hospitality, and good food was part of that. Whenever we spent time together, whether it was Dundee Scotland, London's Soho, New York and San Francisco's Chinatown, we knew that great joy and great adventure were in store for us whenever and wherever we met...Salmon fishing in Victoria, curried or Chinese style Dungeonesse crabs on the West Coast; the oysters and clams, the striped bass we caught off the surf in Cape Cod at twilight, and the simple snails, periwinkles we collected and feasted on with all the skill and love that we recalled from our island home, from our 'boy-days'.

Like most expatriates, we learned how to cook because there were no restaurants that served that kind of cuisine, and worse, there were few places where one could get the right ingredients...fresh water-cress, fresh thyme, chives, callaloo bush, breadfruit and some of the underground roots and tubers that were staples on our island...all of which were impossible to find in London or New York in 1950.

I remember Sam telling how he had a green avocado that was not ready for eating, so he put it in a warm oven hoping to ripen it quickly...one of the failures in an attempt to re-create the past, moving through alien worlds with a yearning for pieces of our lost culture which was losing ground with each year's passing, seeing time like a hungry mouth chewing up the seconds of our lives, seconds which became more and more filled with a sense of alienation and loss...especially when we both crossed that dividing line...you have lived more years of your life abroad than you have lived in the place of your birth, leaving you with the feeling that you have passed the 'point of no return'.

With each visit to the Caribbean we both knew that our 'home', our place of birth had changed, that we came from a past that could never return, the halcyon days of a slow moving tranquil tropical island.

We met in Barbados on our way to Carifesta, the largest festival of the arts held in Guyana in 1972. Sam came from western Canada, I from California. Sam was almost mystical in his belief, his love of the waters of Barbados. It was also a place where we both felt that we could enjoy the Caribbean and its splendors without the baggage of friends and relatives (in Trinidad) friends and relatives with all their problems. We stayed with Lionel Hutchinson, a Bajan novelist who Sam had met in

London in the early fifties. We swam in Bajan waters, ate flying fish and drank Mount Gay Rum, and then we were off to Trinidad...noisy Trinidad, where at night, even if you turned your radio off and pricked up your ears there was a low level sound of the radio station. During the day there was not only the radio, but each main street of the city was flooded with loud music. Each little store had a blaring loudspeaker booming out Calypso or Reggae music, and the same was true of all the mad taxis that plied the main roads of the island. Add to that the heat, the humidity, the sleepness nights swatting mosquitoes, and the rainy season.

We got into one of those 'gypsy' cabs, known for their mad drivers. We squeezed in between its passengers. Sam sat in front, next to the driver. As soon as we entered the cab, I knew that it was the wrong thing to do, the radio was blasting. Sam asked the driver in his usual polite soft-spoken way to turn down the volume. Perhaps the driver did not hear him, maybe he did, but chose to ignore Sam. Again Sam asked him to turn down the volume. This time the driver looked straight at him and sucked his teeth. Sam reached over and turned off the radio. Everyone in the taxi was stunned, both at his action, and the sudden peace and quiet, and we all knew something had to give.

'Stop the car...let me out!' Sam shouted, flinging some crumpled bills at the driver, who promptly pocketed them then turned on the radio again. The rest of us had little time to join him, it all happened so quickly, or were we just cowards?

I saw that lonely disgusted slightly hunched over figure as we drove on. He managed to catch up with us in Port of Spain. All he said in his disgruntled voice was, 'These noisy bastards. Can't stand silence, can't stand the quiet of their own thoughts!'

And the same thing was true in the streets of the city...loudspeakers everywhere, belting and belching out their deafening decibels. Why, I asked myself do we love noise? When did all of this happen? The answer was simple, Sam and I had been away too long. I had seen some of this in other Third World countries. How much we all loved the 'toys' of the electronic world, the play-things of other worlds. When I related this incident to other Trinis they were aghast. What Sam had done could have ended in a fight, a stabbing or shooting...or worse. No one in his right mind would dare to reach over and turn off a radio in a taxi.

'But Sam...you bold you know.' I said.

'Bold my arse...these bastards gone and ruin this place. No peace anywhere anymore...just noise, noise, noise. What ever happen to silence?', he said, not in anger, but more of a wistful longing for a time that was, and was gone forever, the time of our 'boy-days', the halcyon times of Trinidad...lost forever, replaced by something like a caged animal that had been set loose.

After a few days in Trinidad, we flew to Guyana and landed in the middle of a tropical rain storm. The tarmac was flooded, the rain came down too fast to run off. We were met by people with large unbrellas bearing the logo of the air-line which promptly blew inside out. I think that some kind of reception was planned, but no one was interested. It occurred to me that I had never seen rainfall like this in my life. I had seen snow. I had seen hail stones. I had seen sleet, and I had seen many a rainy season on our small island. This was what a rainfall was like in a continent, for we were now on the South American continent, a huge land mass compared to our island home. The skies seemed to burst open through the great lightning bolts and the torrential rains came pouring through the great flashes of dark and open skies. We were soaked and water was running out of our shoes. The cool air-conditioned terminal was no relief, I began to shiver in my wet clothes and longed for a dry place.

One of the things about living in the tropics is that lighting a fire to keep warm, or to dry out is out of the question where it was already ninety degrees. I now wondered about the serene days of my childhood when playing in the rain was such great fun, such great sport.

There were cars waiting for us, and we were driven to a complex of houses, a small city, built especially to house the artists from the entire Caribbean. The first thing on our minds was to get into some dry clothes, and to get some sleep, it was about two in the morning. We no sooner turned off the lights when the mosquitoes descended. They were the largest I had ever seen. Or, had I forgotten what they were like when I was growing up in Trinidad? There were mosquito nets hung over the beds, and one had to make sure that one or two did not get in while one crept into bed with a feeling of 'at last', a bed, while we listened to the heavy pounding and pinging of the galvanised roof. What a wonderful sound that used to be as a child. I wondered what happened to the music the rain used to make as I lay in bed, wide awake, damp and tired. My wife went off to sleep immediately, and I could hear Shake Keen snoring. I wanted to smoke, but that would be difficult under the mosquito netting, so I tossed and turned, and then I heard Sam say, 'You up?'. I merely grunted, then he went out on the porch to smoke, and I joined him. There was a silence between us that spoke of fatigue, lack of sleep, and a feeling of what on earth we were doing in this place. We got back in our beds, and I saw Sam pull the sheets over his head as he lay like a corpse. We said good night again and tried for sleep. I do not know how long I slept, I do not know if I slept, but I was awakened by blaring music coming from a long shed which was put up for the festivities. It had a row of food stalls at either end, and a juke box, I later learned. The light of day came up very early, the rain had cleared away. The first blast of the juke box made us jump, and I could see Sam putting on his clothes, wordlessly. He went into the kitchen where there was a cutlass. I went to the porch to see where he was headed as he slouched to the shed.

I hardly thought that he would hurt anyone with it. But visions of Sam slashing the electric cord, sparks flying...this un-mechanically minded genius would never think to simply un-plug the juke box...and then the music stopped suddenly and I saw him coming back, cutlass in hand. He crawled back into bed and again pulled the covers over his head. 'Everything alright?' I asked. All he said was, 'These noisy bastards.'

The following morning at breakfast in the shed he was laughing and joking with the men who had respected his wish to turn off the juke box. His temper was cooled, and perhaps in part by the large serving of Cascadura, large and plentiful around Guyana's capital, Georgetown which is below sea-level and latticed by rivulets which ebb and flow with the tides of the ocean...perfect breeding for Cascadura...and mosquitoes.

Since there were four of us, Sam, myself and my wife and the poet Shake Keen (from St. Vincent) we were given a house to ourselves, and since we were four, we were given a car with our own chauffeur, around the clock. I have a picture of Sam sitting behind the wheel of the car, smiling that impish smile of his. The humor behind the picture lay in the fact that Sam had never learned how to drive. And while on the subject of the car and the chauffeur, it was Sam, who seeing the man sitting outside in the heat of the car, and who did not want him to feel like a 'servant' went out and fetched him. He was to join us in all of our activities, he was to have his meals and drinks with us, and our house was the most frequented...we had visitors night and day.

At another time, Sam had come to the US, one of the requirements of being a recipient of a Guggenheim grant. I was at Cape Cod for the Summer. After a week or two at the Mc.Dowell Colony, he joined us at the Cape where we had rented a sprawling barn-house overlooking the bay in North Truro. One evening at sunset we were at the pier in Provincetown and the sky was filled with kites...kites such as we had never seen in our lives, not in our 'boy-days'. Sam wanted to be part of that action. He decided that we would build a Mad Bull, a giant one which stood four feet high when finished. All of the kites we had seen were probably bought...ready-made. Ours would be singular in design, and was made by our own hands. We found some bamboo strips in a Japanese gift shop where we also found the right kind of paper. We got some heavy string, and tore up strips from a bed sheet for its tail. We worked at the frame each day, wondering as always if it would fly. And then came the time for choosing and fitting the paper into the empty spaces of the frame. We needed glue, and had none, but Sam remembered how to make a good paste boiling flour in water. Now he needed lime or lemon juice for the paste. I wondered, until he reminded me of how the many bugs at home would eat the kite paper...because of the paste. The addition of the lime juice would make it distasteful to them. I took about a week to finally finish the kite. We were like painters

working on a canvas...so much today, quit to let it dry, then move on to
the other spaces. Meantime, neither of us had given any thought to
transporting it to Provincetown, some four or five miles from Truro. We
tried to get the kite inside the car...head-first, side-ways ever so gently,
but it would not fit, so I drove, and Sam held the kite outside the car as
we drove to the pier where we created quite a stir, and again his twinkle
and impish grin came on, transporting him back to the years of our 'boy-
days' as he explained to the curious onlookers the nature and origin of
the MADBULL, emphasizing the fact that it was not 'store-bought' but
made by hand...from scratch. My chief concern was, will it fly. If it didn't,
it would take a dive...right into the sea. We got set with me holding the
kite in an upright position, its long tail trailing as we waited for a great
gust of wind. 'Leggo' (let-go) I heard him yell, and up went the kite,
straight as an arrow. 'Like a bullet!' I heard him shout as the kite danced
and buzzed, climbing into the sky with each tug of the string. The kite
was called a MADBULL because of the sound it made when in flight.
There were small sections of loose paper that fluttered like wings as the
kite moved through the air, 'singing' as we called it, its song. Each
evening we spent some time patching or strengthening sections of the
kite for the following day's flying.

And then as the summer was drawing to an end, we began to wonder
what we would do with the kite. I thought that we should just cut the
string on the last day and let it wander off to sea. But Sam feared, and he
was almost paranoid about it...that someone would find its frame at sea,
and 'learn' its secret, his secret, and so we did not cut it loose. Sam
crushed it to pieces on the beach the day before we left so that no one
could duplicate his masterpiece.

In all of this, one may well wonder if we did not have any difference of
opinion. We never talked about writing, his, mine, or the works of others
our age. Yet, we did have differing views, views which we both knew
would never be reconciled, and so we treated them as we treated each
other, with mutual respect. We never had any heated dragged out
arguments about them, yet they would surface from time to time.

One of the things we disagreed on was what I refer to as 'identity', a
term I use when asked what my writing is all about. At a conference at
York University to celebrate the 150th. year of the presence of East
Indians in the Caribbean we were on the novelists' panel with four or
five other writers. Frank Birbalsingh, writer, critic, professor and
organiser of the conference was moderator of the panel, and his question
was what we felt our writing was all about. My turn came first. I said
'identity' and went on to explain that I felt that we lived in something of
a borrowed culture, bits and pieces of other peoples' culture. I could tell
that Sam was annoyed, he could not wait to say his piece, and indeed
his tone was an angry one. I cannot recall word for word what he said,
but it went something like this as he broke into West Indian dialect. He

did not address me directly, his comments were directed to Frank, who had asked the question. He said, 'Well...I don't know what that word means, but what I know is that I know who I am...I know what I write about, and all this talk about identity, or exile (another term of disagreement) I am not an exile...Napoleon was exiled. I was not'.

We had lunch after the panel and we never got to re-hash or to clarify just what we felt or meant, instead, we talked about our 'boy-days'.

I recall Sam telling about employment, or looking for work when he first got to England. He, like myself, thinking ourselves to be Indian, thought that a good place to look, some Indian business or agency would be a good place to look for work. Sam told about meeting with Krishna Menon at the Indian Embassy. Menon, even before interviewing him said something like this to him: 'You people from the West Indies seem to feel that you are Indians, that India owes you something. You know nothing of Indian culture or ways, few of you speak our languages etc. etc'. Needless to say he did not get a job with the Indian Embassy despite his qualifications as a journalist, poet, novelist and dramatist.

I also had turned to, not the Embassy, but the UN Delegation which was in the same building as the Embassy. I had heard of a messenger's job with the delegation to the UN, and one of the reasons for looking to the UN Delegation was because I was on a foreign student's visa, which meant that I was not allowed to work in the US, unless the funds came from some non US source. I did get the messenger job for the Summer, but I cannot say that I was treated with the same courtesies that other Indians were treated with. I too, perhaps in more subtle ways was made to understand that I was not Indian, and was looked upon as some sort of anomaly or freak. It was also suggested that I change my name from 'Khan', a muslim name to a Hindu name. One member of the delegation (I had to deliver the morning newspapers and the mail to the delegates in their hotel rooms) seeing me for the first time addressed me in Hindi.I muttered, I stuttered. I did understand him, but I knew that I could not hold a conversation with him in Hindi. Like most second generation people, I understood what my parents were saying, but replied in English. He then proceeded to tell me that although there were many things - facial structure, color or complexion - all of which were clearly Indian, he could tell from the way I walked...just the few steps into his suite...that I did not walk like Indian people, and this was said in the most cutting manner.

Perhaps I use the word 'identity' in my own specific way, however, I was, as Sam was, if not in our writing, coming to terms with who we were, with our sense of 'identity'. It could also be argued that living abroad forces one to see oneself in a different light - not only the way in which we see ourselves, but the way(s) in which others see us.

Living abroad is one thing. Living abroad as a foreign student in the US is another. And living abroad trying to earn enough money to support a family and still have the time and energy to write is still another matter. What artist does not know the joys and sorrows of that life? Yes, there were glorious days; the acceptance of a novel or short story by a publisher, a good review, a luncheon paid for by one's publisher, and the thought or feeling that you would like to ask for a 'doggie bag' to take home the 'left-overs' to your wife and child. And there were other lean mean days.

I remember Sam telling about going through the cold London fog to borrow five pounds from George Lamming. Apparently neither George nor Sam could afford the luxury of a telephone, so he had to take his chances of finding him home. He, Sam, and his family lived in what I believe is called a 'bed-sitter', one room whose only source of heat was a gas ring. I believe it was also used to cook their meals. After he got the five pounds, he then had to worry about finding some shop or store which might still be open so that he could make change...get shillings to insert in the gas meter. One did not go up to strangers in the middle of the night to ask them to change a five pound note. Indeed, I recall him telling how people shunned you because they knew that you wanted shillings and they wanted to hold on to theirs, and here is the way he put it, 'Boy...people see you comin', and sometimes they turn away or look away because they see a black man. It's as if some of them know that you want to make change, some of them just frighten...but nobody want to part with their shillings'.

As it turned out, he had to get some food for himself and his family and was able to get the shillings to take home to keep his family warm...and fed.

I was able to share one of my lean mean days with him. My wife and I and our little girl lived in a tenement on the upper East Side of NYC. While I could work full time for the delegation during that summer, once school resumed I was allowed to work twenty hours a week, which I did, putting away books in the library of the school I attended. We were often broke, with no one to turn to for a loan. And this was not because we did not have friends, it was because all the people we knew were as broke as we were. One day my wife and I decided to walk the streets of the city...to look for money. We found one dime, one penny, and an un-used ten cent stamp. I could also tell tales of washing my clothes in the kitchen bath-tub with its lion's claws, clothes which should have been dry cleaned. The rent for the apartment was thirty dollars a month, a steal and a find in those days, impossible nowadays. Today, I still wonder how I got as much done as I did. I wrote most of my first novel in that apartment. I did not have to worry about the cost of typewriter ribbons or paper, I wrote by hand on the cheapest yellow pulp paper which now disintegrates at the touch of the hand.

Although Sam lived on one side of the Atlantic, and I on the other in NYC (he later moved to Western Canada,I, to California, then back to

NYC) we kept each other informed of everything that went on in our lives through our letters. And then when we met, we were able to do a different kind of catching up going over face to face what we had said in our letters. We were like those two sages in an old joke who sat under a tree. They both knew everything that the other did. As time went by, they felt that there was no need for elaborate communication. They both knew all the same things, all the same stories, all the same jokes. And so, instead of telling each other some joke, in so many words, one of them would shout, 'Joke number one hundred and fifty-five.' And the other, knowing the joke would burst out in peals of laughter, and this is one way, one analogy to describe how close we were, or how well we knew each other.

But there were details that we did not know about our backgrounds. I knew my grand-parents on both sides of my family, I knew what part of India they came from. Sam did not know as much as I did about his ancestors. He was not clear about his father's background, how he came by the name Selvon. He knew that his father, an East Indian had come to Trinidad from Martinique, and he guessed that the name Selvon must have come from French origins. But what was it derived from?

During one of his visits with me at Cornell University, I took him to one of those gala dinners that the Indian Students' Association was giving for one of their major professors. One of the Indian students was familiar with the major Indian languages, and so I introduced him to Sam, and we posed the question to him. Was there some Indian name he could think of that could be the origins of Selvon? He thought that the name could have been 'Salwan'.

Some time later while I was still working on my first novel, I needed a name for a particularly annoying character, a lawyer who I named Mr. Salwan. We both had a good laugh about it, and to this day it remains a private joke, just between us two. It was the kind of joke, if it can be called a joke, that we both loved, and there were times when I did indeed address him 'Salwan'.

His mother was white, or half white, the daughter of Scottish or English estate overseers, and whose maiden name was Dixon (Sam's middle name) led Sam to look into her ancestry. He told of discovering that there was a castle somewhere in England or Scotland to which he was legal heir and planned to show up at its moat one day to lay claim to his inheritance. I think he liked the image more than the fact of carrying out his threat, while I, on the other hand had an image taken no doubt from Don Quixote. I doubt that he carried out his threat, it was much more fun to merely speculate on it.

There are two aspects of Sam's work that are highly praised; his sense of humor and his use of dialect, and we never spoke about them. I do not think that his was a reasoned rational choice, it simply was. Indeed he spoke in Trinidadian dialect, no matter what the situation or occasion. I did the same with the use of dialect despite the rejections and (bad) advice from publishers and friends, who felt that, 'Dialect is hard on the reader'. 'Dialect will slow down the reader.' 'You may find that you will need a glossary at the end of the novel'. Such were the comment and criticism, but we persisted.

For myself, I have wondered about the ability to recall, to re-create the pidgin of Trinidad. Sam was first married to a Guyanese, and it is possible that he and his wife spoke in dialect among themselves. I, on the other hand, was not married to, nor lived with someone from the Carribean. Yet, after forty years, I can, as Sam could, shift from Standard English to pidgin, and I still wonder about the magic of language. I recall a conversation with Austin Clarke (Barbadian novelist who now lives in Toronto) who had apparently made some attempts to write in 'Bajan' dialect. He told me some years ago how he used to go to Sam's work, and mine, trying to figure out how we did it, how he could get into using dialect. He finally gave up, yet he too wondered how anyone living abroad for so many years could still recall and re-create all the subtlety; the nuances and rhymes of our dialect, and finally how to present them so that they did not 'slow down the reader', so that they did not seem labored and over-worked, so that one would not need a glossary at the end of the novel.

Sam may well have been surrounded by West Indians all those years...The Lonely Londoners. I do not have any West Indian friends to speak of. My only West Indian friend and colleague is Lloyd Brown who lives in Los Angeles, he is a poet and scholar and originally from Jamaica. I have had to ask that foolish question that semanticists and psychologists ask all the time. 'What language do you dream in?'. I do not have an answer, and Sam couldn't care less. He was the only person with whom I could slip into Trinidadian dialect, except for those times when I visit the Caribbean where it would sound pretentious to sport an English or American accent...which would be difficult anyway because we all have vestiges of our homeland's pidgin in our speech.

Although I was plagued by questions of this kind that had to do with language or dialect, Sam never was. Of if he was, we never dwelt upon it. We would sometimes surprise each other - with some pleasure - of some long forgotten word or term we grew up with, like the word 'Io'. I had said that when we got done with the MADBULL, we could 'Io' the kite...cut the string and let it sail away, and I still wonder where the Trinis got that word. Sam, who loved to play Scrabble, and who played the game with a dictionary to check out other players, or prove the legitimacy of his words pointed out that 'Io' was a good word, one to be found in the dictionary. Its meaning is as follows: a. A cry of pleasure or triumph. b. A Greek Mythological figure, a maiden loved by Zeus. c. In chemistry an abbreviation for the chemical Ionium. And there are many other words perhaps taken from French or Spanish that had worked their way into the pidgin of Trinidad. I do not know to this day where the word 'chook' came from. It means to stick, to prick with a pin. In one of his later novels he used that word and had to put up a great battle with his publishers, insisting that although 'chook' was not in the dictionary, it was the writer's way of bringing new life to an ongoing language. We now see the word 'chook' in print.

The other much praised aspect of his work is his sense of humor and his use of it. He found humor in the simple, the ordinary, the plain. And he did so because he was a funny man himself. There are those who feel that he laughed at others - at their expense, but I do not think that that was so. His ability to laugh, talk, joke and listen to the people he immortalised was a genuine one. If he laughed, he laughed *with* them because he felt one with them, and he knew them well.

On one of our visits to Trinidad, we were supposed to do a reading at a bookstore in San Fernando, his home-town. The crowd was too large to hold it in the book store, so the reading was held in the Public Library. We found seats and after the opening speaker's remarks, the lights were lowered. When they went back up, the podium had been changed into a stage - with no props, just a couple of actors. As a surprise to Sam, and us, the audience, they began to do a skit based upon one of Sam's short stories from *Ways of Sunlight* The entire house roared, and there was Sam, looking at, listening to his lines, now memorized and delivered with what must have pleased him, he was rolling with laughter. The skit was based upon 'Brackley and the Bed'...filled with all the pathos and humor of the lost and lonely West Indian trying to find the meaning of life in chilly London. Rumor has it that a film is being made of *Lonely Londoners*. It has not been released to the best of my knowledge, but I hope that Sam was able to see it or parts of it before he died. He was involved with the writing of the screenplay.

Writers of fiction, dramatists, actors, comedians - all must have something in common - not only in what they do, but the way in which they react to responses from their audiences. For example, we all wonder about the moments that make people laugh or cry because it sometimes happens that people seem to laugh at a moment which seemed to be one of horror, or sadness, and literary critics are quick to point out that *they*, not the writer - know better where the humor lies.

I have heard Sam read from his work many times, and he is one of the few writers I know, who, while reading his own lines became so animated, so funny and witty as to break out in peals of laughter that caused him to stop reading until he could re-compose himself. He seemed to know best where the essence of his humor lay.

His sense of humor in his work is one thing. But what was his sense of humor like? And how much he wished to share this with others. On one of my visits with him in London, I remember poring over the Sunday papers with him, he loved the Flintstones. Not only did he love the

Flintstones, but he wanted to share this with me. I neither like nor dislike the Flintstones, and I said so.

'Boy...how you don't like the Flintstones? You see people driving cars and carts with square wheels...you don't find that sort of thing funny?'

He would go through the comic strip and burst out laughing which I'm sure he would do even if there was no one around. And he laughed at the Flintstones as he did when he read from his own work. At least I had no problem with *his* humor, and I cannot help but remember how much he wanted to share...to explain just why the Flintstones were so funny to him.

I now live in New York - surrounded by a vast West Indian community, I did not plan it this way. The huge immigrations from the Caribbean seem to have followed me to this cold north-land. In the neighbourhood where I teach English at a college heavily populated by West Indian immigrants or their children, I can find black-pudding, mangoes, avocados, breadfruit, cassava, yam, dasheen, water-cress, callaloo bush, okra...and a small Korean fish store where I can buy conch, king fish and red snapper. Perhaps I too will return to the green and warmth of Trinidad. The cascadura often calls, and one day, when I'm ready, I'm sure that I'll find the little creatures in the market stalls, somewhere where reggae blares in the streets, where Trini, Bajan, Jamaican and other dialects compete with each other - because the cascadura of our 'place', of our childhood and our 'boy-days' calls us all.

AUSTIN CLARKE

From: *A Passage Back Home* (1994): A Personal Reminiscence of Samuel Selvon

I cannot remember how old those Sundays were and if the sun had travelled already over the Observation Post in Clapham, and was running over Britton's Hill, down into the Garrison Pasture, before night caught it, to plunge for that day, into Gravesend Beach, and end the light of Sunday. I cannot remember what time it was, when I first heard, either his voice or the magnificent acquainted language of his stories, sent back to us from overseas; and I did not, like all of us, consider it strange or characteristic of our cultural status, that our words spoken amongst us, in fragments and with no force of appeal, would be golden and acceptable portraits of our lives, *because* they were coming to us on these Sunday nights, from overseas: on the BBC's radio programme, *Caribbean Voices*.

My step-father, Police Constable Fitz Herbert Luke, controlled the 'private set,' as he probably controlled the irascible men he had to arrest, with a wrist-lock, making their movements conform to his own obsessive views of obedience and order and lawfulness. And even if he could not precisely define these characteristics he had learned in the Barbados Police Force, (not yet 'Royal'!), and in his own upbringing, I was not too small not to know that he meant those criminals were lacking in 'Christian-mindedness.' And this could be achieved only by listening to the sermons that came all day long, every Sunday, over the 'private set,' from the Andes Mountains. Luckily, we had passed that chapter that dealt with South American geography in the text-book written by Dudely Stampp, at Combermere School. I would be entranced as he was, sitting in the front house, with the cold glass of lemonade, in a color I still cannot describe, with the chipped ice and the pith of the limes, swirling in it, as I listened to the voice and the chastisements and the thunder that summoned Sodom and Gomorrah, that gripped all of us into shuddering submission to those strange voices, those strange arguments, those strange men who through this mechanical device, the 'private set,' were able to enter our houses and occupy our minds, and scold us into this Christian-mindedness. My step-father listened to these sermons on Sundays for more hours than I would spend any day at Combermere School.

But luckily for me, a message would come from the Married Women's Quarters, near the Garrison, from Captain Farmer, the Commissioner of Police, that something was wrong, and that 'Mr. Luke was wanted.' There was one telephone in our neighbourhood, the Yarde's; and one of the Yarde-boys would have to walk the message from the Front Road, which all the boys journeyed, to Flagstaff Road.

And I would rejoice. The 'private set' would be mine, after all. My mother's own feeling that we had been remanded from the onslaught of these religious sermons, from ten o'clock until the last leghorn fowl was on her roost, came out like mild blasphemy. 'Praise God! He out o' the house!' She would have had her eyes on the part of the dial which brought Auntie Kay from Trinidad's Golden Network, with its own version of blasphemy over the seas to the sensibilities of Barbadians washed in Sunday properness of behavior. 'Playing tuk! And on a Sunday, to-boot?'; but it was time of year when the new tunes were being tried by the talent of children; and we might be in for some musical wonder. But before the 'tuk, and on a Sunday!' I would be permitted to roll the heavy knob of the ball-bearing tuning button along the waves of miles of the dial, passing countries in Latin America, moving over Holland (the 'private set' was made in Holland!), through Europe's intractable languages, until by accident, I was plunged into the Mother Country. *Inglann!*

And a different kind of 'tuk' would take possession of the air-waves. Caribbean Voices! And this is when I first heard the name, Samuel Selvon of Trinidad. It was, as Oliver Jackman would put it, a literary 'federation' taking place. Our culture of Sundays, regular as our bowels on a first-Sunday; regimented as the dry-peas and rice and baked chicken, sweet potatoes, pear, lemonade and rum-punch, was Rediffusion's recorded church services of ponderous, sonorous sermons delivered by Inglish vicars whose language was not the language of our miseries, and could not determine nor define what was contained in our hearts. They did not even know our sins. Or it would be choirs from Westminster Abbey, with which we joined in, demonstrating our own arrogant belief that Barbadians sang Hymns Ancient and Modern more better than anybody born. Or a chanced taped version of the same hymns, delivered by the men in the neighbourhood, at a Wake or a Sunday 'service o' song.' And of course, the interminable foreign-affairs chastisement coming from over the Andes Mountains, out of foreign mouths.

But to hear, all of a sudden about the breadfruit tree; the casaurinas; the names of flowers we had passed earlier that very Sunday, to and from Sin-Matthias or Sin-Barnabas, or even the Cathedral - those of us who travelled through the Pine, when it still had canes and was a plantation; through Government Hill, and saw them growing over the wall of the Convent - the Kiskides, Couva, Port of Spain, Gravesend Beach and 'Trumper': to hear these symbols of words, greater than words; greater than our recognition of them in everyday life, all this was to make us feel 'we was people, too.'

I cannot say that I understand all, or even most, of what was being transmitted back to me. I cannot say that I understand each poem about Sin-Lucia, Barbados, Guyana and Trinidad, written by men of those 'unknown' lands, who were so similar to me, and others who had passed these monuments in our respective neighbourhoods; the casaurina, the blue seas, the Sea Wall. I could not receive this 'literary tuk' with an easy appetite because I had not been trained with tools that were Barbadian, to criticise it, or what is worse, to appreciate it. But I knew that something revolutionary, some 'damn federation' was happening on those Sunday nights, when my mother and I, leaned close to the magnificent speaker of the linen-clothed mouth of the 'private set' in the front house.

Samuel Selvon of Trinidad was one voice I heard over the radio. His works had appeared earlier, I am sure, in the small, tidy, impressive and clairvoyant pages of *Bim Literary Quarterly*, assembled against greatest odds, money and energy, by Mr Frank Collymore, who taught me English more successfully than he could French, at Combermere School. But apart from that, apart from the privileged peeping into those pages, illustrated sometimes by gargoyles and monsters and 'colly-beases,' we would know of his existence in a more magnified romantic way, in the weekly injections of 'Caribbean Voices.'

My little world of no more than thirty houses on either side of Flagstaff Road, stretching from the Corner where the Kendal Hill bus stopped, to the top of the hill leading down into the Saturday iniquity, as my mother would say, of Club Morgan, a club which catered to the tastes of white people only, and foreigners, and with a view of the commanding sea and ocean, over which earlier Samuel Selvon, along with George Lamming and Derek Walcott, A.N. Forde and others had crossed in this new revolutionary and reversed 'Middle Passage.' There were the thirty or so houses perched on foundations of precarious blocks of coral stone mined by men from the same neighbourhood, with their sleepy windows adorned with rich window blinds of gold and silver, white and pink; this world which before these 'voices,' were littled in their Inglanned sensibilities regarding self, regarding dignity, regarding blackness and the variations of that blackness - lightness considered beyond the meaning of 'lectricity - regarding nationality and nationhood, regarding the new raging men, Cox and Adams; Barrow and Walcott; Mapp and Allder; Mottley and Talma, and others, many others; my world received the injection of those 'voices' which in turn made sense of the diagnosis and the bitter medicine of ex-colonialism that these great men were ranting about, on the political platforms, and in rum shops throughout the island which was no longer small.

How could such magnificent, powerful brains be contained in only one hundred and sixty-six square miles? How could we have amongst us, such big-brained men in various professions and vocations, the law, medicine, education, philanthropy - and women too - Henderson Clarke, Chris Springer, Mervyn Campbell, Beckles and Madame Ifill, and not wonder at their presence in our midst, and not bestow upon them, the glory and appreciation for this level of achievement measured, not in our own terms, (for we had no way of measuring; we did not measure, but in Inglann's terms? Did not the BBC tell us, even if we were hard-mouthed about accepting this 'federation' truth, that our 'voices' were on the same level as those nurtured in the same Inglann; and that our apprehension of 'fair daffodils,' of Browning's 'In a Gondola,' and Tennyson's 'In Memoriam,' were now so aesthetically special and superior to George Lamming's early poems, (some say he is a better poet than novelist!), and now, for all to see and hear, 'Omeros' by Derek Walcott who does not, thank God, need that validation from the BBC or the *Times Literary Supplement?* And did we not, on the pastures, on the beaches, the playing fields of Combermere, Harrison College, Lodge and Foundation; roads rutted with rock-stone, and any available space, on Sundays, banks holidays and 'in tesses,' see, before anyone else, Foffie Williams, Griff the fass-bowler, numerous Williamses, Smiths of two distinct tribes; Walcotts, Weekes and Worrell, and many others; and many others, still to come - with Sobers, Hall, Hunte, to name a few? And did we not applaud them on Saturday afternoon, forget them on Monday, put them in curing moth-balled neglect and ignoring, until the Inglish came down, and *their* writers told *us* in the language of Oxford and reality, that this was another aspect of our greatness?

Why did we not, until these cricketing 'voices,' bestow upon our greatness our own acclamation? Is it because there are so many great ones that our conservative exuberance for praise was not generous enough to go around? I do not know the answer. But I do know, that the calypsonian, that sharp-eyed historian of our greatness and our weakness understood first, before any Tourist Authority, before any awakened Prime Minister to these axioms of greatness, before any struck committee, the calypsonians our living poets, with their apprehension of contemporary affairs, took notice of the enormity of the *event.* It happened at Lord's, didn't it? Could there be any other stage on earth, on which this dramatization of the battle between a known giant, and a contestant, not unlike the mythical Samson, could be more splendidly acted out? 'Cricket, lovely cricket!' It was spoken, with more literary poignancy than the languorous and sometimes dulcet tone of John Arlott, himself a poet of some consideration. But it remained for our cultural historian, the caisoman, himself a 'Lord,' Lord Kitchener, to draw its historical, its social and its cultural importance to our attention.

This, in another way, is what our 'voices,' pelted back to us on the BBC, and amongst which was Sam's, this is what Sam's voice did to me.

The dramatization of ex-colonialism and the building of a new sensibility, nationalism in its best sense; the disabusing of our minds from the position we had been schooled in: that we had no culture; that we had no models from amongst us, all this was vouchsafed in the language of Samuel Selvon.

There was no way, no fantasy large enough, no expectation that Sam would come into my life as literary model, as literary companion and travelling companion, and as friend, from the first journey of his 'voice' over the BBC.

He had gone, like many immigrants in the fifties, to Inglann, not to be a writer, as most of the commentaries on West Indian writing argue. He had gone to Inglann to make a living, in circumstances perhaps more endurable and sympathetic than he felt he could live with in his Trinidad. He had gone with the grand emigration of men and women looking for work. And if, as he discovered, he was able to work on London's Transport system, in hospitals as an orderly, at the Exchange, and still have time and money to indulge his desire to be a writer; to have the time to dream, and to capture with hair-splitting accuracy *the voice* of Trinidadians and West indians and in a language which today, is being encouraged by academicians in Amurca, in various programmes of Black Studies, and African-American Studies; to put into that language he had heard on the streets throughout Trinidad the ethno-cultural etymology and raise it to a level of beauty, then his emigration was a blessing.

It was a Thursday in 1965, in London, in the Bible of literary justice, the *Times Literary Supplement,* (TLS). On the front page. I can still remember the headline which spanned the breadth of the page, like a panoply over an artist's drawing of a typewriter. *New wine in old Bottles.*

The 'old bottles' was the metaphor for the English language: tired, worn out, stiff, unable to cope with the changing realities of strangers upon the English landscape and their insistence, like the cricketers of Lord Kitchener's 'at Lords,' that there was a new kid on the block, so to say.

The 'new wine' was the literary assault that was being made against the bastion of a 'canon' that had been our measurement, before one brave Englishman, Swanzy brought about this 'federation' of new writing on the BBC's 'Caribbean Voices.' The article praised the contribution of these new batsmen with words, who had injected into a tired way of saying things, the breath of the spice, the glitter and flash of a willow pointing a new ball, or an old ball, through covers; and as John Arlott said many times, about Worrell, about Weekes, about Walcott - and John Goddard - the beauty was in the speed with which the shot had been made, its execution like laser, and 'not a *man* moved.' Or as Shell Harris, in his own beautiful cultural vernacular described it, 'Jesus Christ! Another four!'

The *TLS* article singled out the new great literature batsmen: stroke players of 'Jesus Christ, prettiness!' There were stylists and magicians with the pen, as Ramadhin and Valentine 'those two lil pals of mine,' had done with the little red ball. It singled out Sam Selvon, it singled out George Lamming, it singled out V.S. Naipaul, it singled out Austin Clarke, and it singled out Dylan Thomas. But Sam's identification with this 'new wine,' is what concerns me here. It concerns me now, because, all we have left, after his sudden passing away in the land he loved, in which he was raised, and which he himself raised to an international symbol, through the language he used to describe it, through Trinidad's language, all we have left to do, is sit and read those words that are as invaluable as the calypsoes by Sparrow or Lord Kitchener. I shall not recite any of his words here. I shall not compare any of his stories to those of any other authors. This is not intended to be a comparative criticism. It is simply a personal reminiscence, an appreciation of the wealth he has left behind. The wealth of words heard in the jammed streets of Trinidad, words that paint action, feeling, emotion, death and above all, life. Words that I hear all the time: and heard even before I came face to face with him during this trip to Inglann in 1965.

I was there for the launching of my second novel, *Amongst Thistles and Thorns;* and my publishers, Heinemann, were putting on a party for the occasion. It was a Thursday. The *TLS* had just come out, and we were being praised. I was there also, because I was still a freelance radio broadcaster with the Canadian Broadcasting Corporation; and I had been commissioned to do a three-part radio series on West Indian immigrants in London.

Knowing the role of the artist in the defining of the people from which the artist has come, and among whom he lives, and taking the example of Lord Kitchener, I knew I would have to talk with writers, if I was going to understand the essence of the existence of these West Indians, newcomers, new batsmen upon the severe, grey inhospitable landscape of Inglann and Lords, and London.

Had I not read, 'Waiting for Auntie to Cough,' and pictured myself, through Sam's words palpable as taste, following and imitating the most minute movement of these men through the labyrinths of London and Inglann? It was not difficult to see the improvisation of that immigrant man, whether Trinidadian, Jamaican or Barbadian, who through the exigency of racism or scarce employment opportunity, realising that his own national culture did not put the same emotional value upon the life of a pigeon, flitting over Times Square in droves, and in eaves in greater droves, and spluttering the carefully laundered white shirt - perhaps, the only one - with shit; and knowing that if one was gone, it could not be

missed in such great tragedy as the Inglish are wont to bestow upon the
death of one of their pets. And who, in his right senses, would call a
blasted stray pigeon, a pet! And *feed* him? And starve?

To put it into a 'luminium saucepan, and drop in some lard oil,
pepper, salt and curry - the bane to Inglish noses in the fifties! - and
some rice, and have dinner! And who is more useful, more important, a
West Indian evading death from hunger: or an Inglish pigeon!

In Sam's intention there was not supposed to be this severe, psycho-
literary interpretation, riddled with symbolism. It was the mastery of the
man's usage of language that through its easy comprehension, we, the
reader, the critic and the academician, were able to understand clearly
what he was saying. We read into his words, so clear and single-
minded, all the underlying serious implications that they suggested.

The Lonely Londoners is my favorite among Sam's books. In it I can
smell the perspiration of the labouring West Indians. Can feel their
resentment to their treatment at the hands of the 'Mother.' Can follow
them through the dark, cold, dreary and debilitating alleys on the way to
their ambitions: a Barrister-at-law, a supervisor on London's Transport,
a qualified teacher. And I can hear their pain. And most of all, sense their
nostalgia, and their ambivalence about the wisdom of leaving
Bridgetown or Port of Spain for Inglann. Sam gave me the blue print to
that 'exile,' 'exile' not always so pleasurable as George Lamming
contended it to be in his personal brilliant commentary, *The Pleasures of
Exile*, which dealt with his own life in Inglann.

When I arrived there, armed with a Nagra tape recorder and a huge
per diem account, I was both prepared and unprepared for the blight I
was to live with and in, during those two weeks in Inglann's 'summer.'

But the *TLS* had extolled beforehand, the excellence of this renaissance
of writing, this West Indian literary force that dared to demonstrate the
working-out of the 'new wine' in Inglann's back-yards. George
Lamming was at the height of his fame. V.S. Naipaul has just begun to
court the Inglish and massage them into believing in his own nihilistic
attitude. Jan Carew, living in a large house somewhere near Wimbledon,
clothed in the huge skins of animals slaughtered or found dead,
somewhere on the Steppes of Europe or the Latin American Pampas of
boar-hunting, seal-hunting, or mink-hunting; and flitting from London
to Moscow, and back many times, before the term 'jet-setter' was
invented and thrown into our lexicon. Andrew Salkey, whom I have
christened 'Handrew' in memory of his Jamaican Creole roots, buried
amongst shelves and shelves of books reaching to the heavens in his
prodigious study. Michael Anthony whose hands were calloused, and
made harder, not from the solitary pounding on his manual typewriter,
but from the laborer's job he held, for years, to put bread and butter on
his table for wife and child. James Berry who persevered with poetry.

Sam had captured even the smell of London's winter in his brilliant novel, *The Lonely Londoners*. And he had done something else. He had stripped them of the alienating hyphenation so common these days in the way we describe ourselves as minority ethnic groups living in a land other than our own. He christened them *Londoners*. Not black Londoners. Not Trinidadian-Londoners.Not Black West Indians in London.Just Londoners. And he left it to the other tribes inhabiting that inhospitable landscape, to like it, or lump it. This distinction of definition is significant: for it describes not only the disposition of those brave men and women to the reversed direction of the 'journey,' but more than that, it expresses the ethno-cultural philosophy of the man. Never once, during countless meetings, from 1965 until two years ago when we met at Brock University in St. Catharines, Canada, have I heard, even in jest, a word of implicit racialism come from this man's lips. And in hundreds of letters we exchanged between London and Toranno (Toronto); and later on, between Calgary, Alberta and Toranno, there is no trace of enmity caused by his encounters with racism, (and he had many), that colored his behavior, his life, or his writing.

The House in which Sam lived at this time, was an ordinary house. Not outstanding in any of its dimensions. A house in which the Inglish put its under-class to live. I remember he was wearing a sweater. And smoking. There might have been whiskey. But his circumstances tell me that whiskey could possibly not have been served. I do not remember eating lunch, or being offered any. The starkness of his surroundings and environment was not what I had imagined from his lively fiction in his short stories. This home was more in keeping with the lugubriousness of the life Edgar Mittelholzer wrote about in his autobiography. I could imagine the heavy strains of Wagner, which Edgar liked and listened to without taking a breath. I could imagine the locus of many of Charles Dickens' novels, except that this encounter was in the suburbs. I could imagine the garret and the woolened writer in darkness, no food, and the romantic prop of bottles of red wine, and burning candles drooping from a Chianti bottle whose mouth and basketted sides are drenched in dried tallowed sculptures. Not so this house.

But there was dignity. And humanness. Sam had lots of that. The dignity of simplicity. His words exemplified that. I sat with him, in this minimalized surroundings, there was no music, no oil paintings, and we talked about London and Inglann for hours; and we talked not too successfully about his work and its place in the sphere of the 'new-wined' renaissance of West indian letters. And his self-effacing nature was the ethic, the nature and the essence of the interview. I think I asked Sam about his colleagues. Especially Naipaul, who had just made a mark for himself in world literature, if we may describe his success, in those terms. *A House for Mr. Biswas,* perhaps his best novel, had just been published to great acclaim. But there was a problem. Was Naipaul really the son of a bitch that Handrew had hinted at? It was Handrew, after all,

who had introduced Naipaul to his publishers André Deutsch. And it
was Naipaul, with the large publisher's cheque against advanced
royalties, who could no longer remember Handrew's address on
Moscow Road, London. Was all the rumor I was hearing, true? Were the
recriminations about V.S. Naipaul, his nihilistic attitude towards black
people, spread by his former friends, justified? I was convinced of his
tremendous technical ability with the novel. I had not been able to
separate this genius with structure, from the contents of his non-fiction,
in particular, *The Middle Passage*. And years later, when he gave us the
big book on his return to India, with the motto of Indian personality,
"The Indian defecates everywhere. He defecates on the street, in his temples..." I
asked Sam what he felt about *An Area of Darkness*, in which this nihilistic
brand of satire appeared. I was expecting a personal commentary from a
fellow Trinidadian. Something, though not so spiteful as the censure I
had met, when the same question had been asked of other West Indian
writers, the young nationalist intellectuals, and university students who
did not necessarily read nor study Naipaul in their English curriculums
– but something spicy. Perhaps, I was waiting to hear the latest personal
gossip, to be able to bury this out-standing, money-making fellow
author. Perhaps, it was too, nothing but plain envy and jealousy. For
none of us had had Naipaul's wide and international attention. Not even
George Lamming. Not Eddie Brathwaite. And not, most certainly at that
time, Derek Walcott.

I sat back, rubbing my two palms together, sipping the rum - or was
it beer served too warm, which I do not like - waiting for the avalanche
of what I felt would be justified disapprobrium.

Sam sipped his drink. Took a pull on the cigarette which was always
in his mouth. And he said, in his voice that was so comforting in its
soothing quality, like the voice of a dramatic actor who loves comedy; in
a voice like a clown's, and the best of classical clowns, filled with
wisdom beneath the humor; Sam said, *"Boy, Vidia is Vidia, yuh know.
Vidia does-do his thing and thing, and that is Vidia. I ain't know nothing, eh
boy. I does-do my thing, and Vidia does-do his thing. Is so, yuh know, boy..."*

There was no enmity, no jealousy, no recrimination. There was no hint
of wanting to be in Vidia's shoes, and share in the enormous advances
and prize money he had been having, no regret that he was not on the
BBC television shows which lionized his countryman; no word of
censure against the recognition given to Naipaul, in such large measure
that it was felt in Inglann at the time, that Vidia was the only author
worth noticing.

It taught me the essence about Sam, this great man, 'no longer
whinnying with us,' as Dylan Thomas would have couched the words of
his panegyric, had he too been alive, and had he not succumbed to the
record-breaking transitory fame of drinking scotches. 'I think this is a
record,' Dylan is supposed to have said, when he drank others under the

table, and himself, into the lamented coffin. *'Do not go gentle into that good night.'* It could have been said about Sam's passing in Trinidad on the 17th of April, as it was said about the passing of Dylan's own father. I did not expect to see Sam in this state and status. Meeting him, there was not the same dignity and magnificence that his prose had portrayed for me all those years before; his home was not distinguished in the way that his fiction's language had succeeded in distinguishing the English language. And I knew that the time he had taken away from his typewriter to talk to me, was golden. There was no wife at home. I do not know if I knew he had a wife in those days. But he probably had. For I think I remember there was a child, an infant. The voice was coming from a room I could not see. I knew, from what my eyes passed over, in his castle, that there were no T-bone steaks on Fridays, and roast beef and Yorkshire puddings on Sundays. That sherry was not served at five in the afternoon. That the car was not taken out in the Sunday evening dying sun, and driven into the country. I know that that time, all the time available, had to be spent over the laboring Underwood typewriter, and that late into the night, at the hour when even graveyards are quiet, that the working wife, and the infant, would hear the clacking-out of words in the new language he was fashioning into the 'new wine' of the Inglish canon that determined the modern novel.

SAM SELVON

Calypsonian (1952)
for Errol Hill

It had a time when things was really brown in Trinidad, and he couldn't make a note nohow, no matter what he do, everywhere he turn, people telling him they ain't have work. It look like if work scarce like gold, and is six months now he ain't working.

He owe everybody. He have a dollar for Mavis, he have three shillings for Conks (he see good hell to get that three shillings off Conks), and he have twelve cents for Man Centipede.

Besides that, he owe Chin parlour about five dollars, and the last time he went in for a sandwich and a sweetdrink, Chin tell him no more trusting until he pay off all he owe. Chin have his name in a copybook under the counter.

'Wait until the calypso season start,' he tell Chin, 'and I go be reaping a harvest. You remember last year how much money I had?'

But though Chin remember last year, that still ain't make him soften up, and it reach a position where he hungry, clothes dirty, and he see nothing at all to come, and this time so, the calypso season about three four months off.

On top of that, rain falling nearly every day, and the shoes he have on have big hole in them, like if they laughing, and the water getting up in the shoes and have his foot wet.

One day he get so damn disgusted he take off the shoes and walk barefoot all in Frederick Street and Charlotte Street, and people looking at him as if he mad, but he don't give a blast.

Was the rain what cause him to tief a pair of shoes from a shoemaker shop in Park Street. Is the first time he ever tief, and it take him a long time to make up his mind. He stand up there on the pavement by this shoemaker shop, and he thinking things like, oh God when I tell you I hungry, and all the shoes around the table, on the ground, some capsize, some old and some new, some getting halfsole and some getting new heel.

It have a pair just like the one he have on.

The table cut up for so, as if the shoemaker blind and cutting the wood instead of the leather, and it have a broken calabash shell with some boil starch in it. The starch look like pap; he so hungry he feel he could eat it.

Well, the shoemaker in the back of the shop, and it only have few people sheltering rain on the pavement. It look so easy for him to put down the old pair and take up another pair - this time so, he done have his eye fix on a pair that look like Tecnic, and just his size, too besides.

He remember how last year he was sitting pretty - two-tone Tecnic, gabardeen suit, hot tie. Now that he catching his royal, everytime he only making comparison with last year, thinking in his mind how them was the good old days, and wondering if they go ever come back again.

And it look to him as if tiefing could be easy, because plenty time people does leave things alone and go away, like how now the shoemaker in the back of the shop, and all he have to do is take up a pair of shoes and walk off in cool blood.

Well it don't take plenty to make a tief. All you have to do is have a fellar catching his royal, and can't get a work noway, and bam! By the time he make two three rounds he bounce something somewhere, an orange from a tray, or he snatch a bread in a parlour, or something. Like how he bounce the shoes.

So though he frighten like hell and part of him going like a pliers, he playing victor brave boy and whistling as he go down the road. The only thing now is that he hungry. Right there by Queen Street in front a Chinee restaurant, he get an idea. Not an idea in truth all he did think was: in for a shilling in for a pound. But when he think that, is as if he begin to realise that if he going to get stick for the shoes, he might as well start tiefing black is white.

It had a time he used to tell the boys so. He used to say, ' It don't make no sense going to jail for tiefing twenty dollar, you might as well tief couple thousand.'

So he open now to anything; all you need is a start, all you need is a crank up, and it come easy after that.

What you think he planning to do? He planning to walk in the Chinee restaurant and sit down and eat a major meal, and then out off without paying. It look so easy, he wonder why he never think of it before. The waitress come up while he looking at the menu. She stand up there, with a pencil stick up on she ears like a real test, and ...he realize that this restaurant work only part-time as far as she concern, because she look as if she sleepy, she body bend up like a piece of copper wire.

What you go do? She must be only getting a few dollars from the Chinee man, and she can't live on that. He realize suddenly that he bothering about the woman when he himself catching his tail, so he shake his head and watch down at the menu. He made to order a portion of everything. Fry rice, chicken chop-suey, roast pork, chicken chow-min, bird-nest soup, chicken broth, and one of them big salad with big slice of tomato and onion.

He began to think again about the last calypso season, when he was holding big, and used to go up by the high-class Chinee restaurant in St

Vincent Street. He think how is a funny thing how sometimes you does have so much food that you eat till you sick, and another time you can't even see you way to hustle a rock and mauby.

It should have some way that when you have the chance you could eat enough to last you for a week or a month, and he make a plan right there, that the next time he have money (oh God) he go make a big deposit in a restaurant, so that all he have to do is walk in and eat like stupidness.

But the woman getting impatient. She say, ' You taking a long time to make up you mind, like you never eat in a restaurant before.'

And he think about the time when he had money, how no frowsy woman could have talk to him so. He remember how them waitresses used to hustle to serve him, and one night the talk get around that Razor Blade the Calypsonian was in the place, and they insist that he give them a number. Which one it was again? The one about Home and the Bachelor.

Come come, make up you mind, mister, I have work to do.

So he order plain boil rice and chicken stew, because the way how he feeling, all them fancy Chinee dish is only joke, he feel as if he want something like roast breadfruit and saltfish, something solid so when it go down in you belly you could feel it there.

And he tell the woman to bring a drink of Barbados rum first thing, because he know how long they does take to bring food in them restaurant, and he could coast with the rum in the meantime. When he begin to coast with the rum, his head feel giddy, because is a long time since he hit a rum, and his stomach surprise when it feel the liquor. Every two three thoughts he have, he thinking oh God with them, as if oh God is something that must go with everything. Like: oh God them was good days. And, oh God it making hot today.

By the time the food come he feeling so hungry he could hardly wait, he fall down on the plate of rice and chicken as if is the first time he see food, and in three minute everything finish. He drink two glass of ice water, and he pick up a matchstick from the ground and begin to pick his teeth, and he lean back in the chair. And is just as if he seeing the world for the first time, he feel like a million, he feel like a lord; he gave a loud belch and bring up some of the chicken and rice to his throat; when he swallow it back down it taste sour.

He thinking how it had a time an American fellar hear a calypso in Trinidad and he went back to the States and he get it set up to music and thing, and he get the Andrew Sisters to sing it, and the song make money like hell, it was on Hit Parade and all; wherever you turn, you only hearing people singing that calypso. This time so, the poor calypsonian who really write the song catching hell in Trinidad: it was only when some smart lawyer friend tell him about copyright and that sort of business that he wake up. He went to America; and how you don't know he get a lot of money after the case did fix up in New York?

Razor Blade know the story good; whenever he write a calypso, he always praying that some big-shot from America would hear it and like it, and want to set it up good. The Blade used to go in Frederick Street and Marine Square by the one two music shops, and look at all the popular songs, set up in notes and words, with the name of the fellar who wrote it big on the front, and sometimes his photograph too. And Razor Blade used to think: but why I can't write song like that too, and have my name all over the place?

And when things was good with him, he went inside now and then, and tell the clerks and them that he does write calypsos. But they only laugh at him, because they does think calypso is no song at all, that what is song is numbers like 'I've Got You Under My Skin' and ' Sentimental Journey', what real American composers write.

And the Blade used to argue that every dog has his day, and that a time would come when people singing calypso all over the world like stupidness. He thinking about all that as he lean back there in the Chinee man restaurant. Is to peel off now without paying? The best way is to play brassface, do as if you own the damn restaurant, and walk out cool.

So he get up and he notice the waitress not around (she must be serving somebody else), and he take time and walk out, passing by the cashier who writing something in a book. But all this time, no matter how boldface you try to be, you can't stop part of you from going like a pliers, a clip clip, and he feel as if he want to draw his legs together and walk with two foot as one.

When the waitress find out Razor Blade gone without paying, she start to make one set of noise, and a Chinee man from the kitchen dash outside to see if he could see him, but this time so Razor Blade making races down Frederick Street.

The owner of the restaurant tell the woman she have to pay for the food that Razor Blade eat, that was she fault, and she begin to cry big water, because is a lot of food that Razor Blade put away, and she know that that mean two three dollars from the salary.

This time so, Razor Blade laughing like hell; he quite down by the railway station, and he know nobody could catch him now.

One set of rain start to fall suddenly. Razor Blade walking like a king in his new shoes, and no water getting up in his foot this time, so he ain't even bothering to shelter. And he don't know why, but same time he get a sharp idea for a calypso. About how a man does catch his royal when he can't get a work no way. The calypso would say about how he see some real hard days; he start to think up words right away as he walking in the rain.

It had a time in this colony
When everybody have money excepting me
I can't get a work no matter how I try

It look as if good times pass me by.

He start to hum it to the tune of an old calypso (Man Centipede: ' Bad Too Bad'), just to see how it shaping up. And he think about One Foot Harper, the only one man who could help him out with a tune. Every time when he think of a calypso, he used to go round by One Foot, who was one of them old tests surviving from the old days when calypso first start up in Trinidad. And One Foot used to help him with the tune.

It had a big joke with One Foot one time. Somebody tief One Foot crutch one day when he was catching a sleep under a weeping willow tree in Woodford Square, and One Foot had to stay in the square for a whole day and night. You could imagine how he curse stink; everybody only standing up and laughing like hell; nobody won't lend a hand, and if wasn't for Razor Blade, now so One Foot might still be waiting under the weeping willow tree for somebody to get a crutch for him.

But the old Blade help out the situation, and since that time, the both of them good friends.

So Razor Blade start making a tack for the tailor shop which part One Foot does always be hanging out, because One Foot ain't working noway, and every day he there by the tailorshop, sitting down on a soapbox and talking balls whole day.

But don't fret your head. One Foot ain't no fool; it had a time in the old days when they used to call him King of Calypso, and he was really good. If he did have money, or education business, is a sure thing he would have been up the ladder, because he was the first man who ever had the idea that calypsonians should go away and sing in America and England. But people only laugh at One Foot when he say that.

Razor Blade meet One Foot in a big old talk about the time when the town hall burn down. (One Foot was saying he know the fellar who start the fire). When One Foot see him, he stop arguing right away, and he say, ' What happening paleets, long time no see?'

Razor Blade say, 'Look man, I have a sharp idea for a calypso. Let we go in the back of the shop and work it out.'

But One Foot feeling comfortable on the soapbox. He say, 'Take ease, don't rush me. What about the shilling you have for me, that you borrow last week?'

The Blade turn his pockets inside out, and a pair of dice roll out, and a penknife fall on the ground.

' Boy, I ain't have cent. I broken. I bawling. If you stick me with a pin you won't draw blood.'

' Don't worry with that kind of talk, is so with all you fellars, you does borrow a man money and then forget his address.'

' I telling you man,' Razor Blade talk is if he in a hurry, but is only to get away from the topic, ' you don't believe me?'

But the Foot cagey. He say, ' All right, but I telling you in front that if you want money borrow again, you come to the wrong man. I ain't lending you a nail till you pay me back that shilling that you have for me.' The Foot move off the soapbox, and stand up balancing on the crutch.

' Come man, do quick.' Razor Blade make as if to go behind the shop in the backroom. Same time he see Rahamut, the Indian sailor.

' What happening Indian, things looking good with you?'

Rahamut stop stitching a khaki pants and look at the Blade.

' You and One Foot always writing calypso in this shop, all-you will have to give me a commission.'

' Well you know how it is, sometimes you up, sometimes you down. Right now I so down that bottom and I same thing.'

' Well old man is a funny thing, but I never see you when you up.'

' Ah, but wait till the calypso season start.'

' Then you won't come round here at all. Then you is bigshot, you forget small fry like Rahamut.'

Well Razor Blade don't know what again to tell Rahamut, because is really true all what the Indian saying about he and One Foot hanging out behind the shop. And he think about these days when anybody tell him anything, all he could say is, ' Wait till the calypso season start up,' as if when the calypso season start up God go come to earth, and make everybody happy.

So what he do is he laugh kiff-kiff and give Rahamut a pat on the back like they is good friends.

Same time One Foot come up, so they went and sit down by a break-up table.

Razor Blade say, ' Listen to these words old man, you never hear calypso like this in you born days,' and he start to give the Foot the words.

But from the time he start, One Foot chook his fingers in his ears and bawl out, ' Oh God old man, you can't think up something new, is the same old words every year.'

'But how you mean man,' the Blade say, 'this is calypso father. Wait until you hear the whole thing.'

They begin to work on the song, and One Foot so good that in two-twos he fix up a tune. So Razor Blade pick up an empty bottle and a piece of stick, and One Foot start beating the table, and is so they getting on, singing this new calypso that they invent.

Well Rahamut and another Indian fellar who does help him out with the sewing come up and listen.

' What you think of this new number, papa?' the Blade ask Rahamut .

Rahamut scratch his head and say, ' Let me get that tune again.'

So they begin again, beating on the table and the bottle, and Razor Blade imagine that he singing to a big audience in the Calypso Tent, so he putting all he have in it.

When they finished the fellar who does help Rahamut say, ' That is hearts.'

But Rahamut say, ' Why you don't shut your mouth? What all-you Indian know about calypso?'

And that cause a big laugh, everybody begin to laugh kya-kya, because Rahamut himself is an Indian.

One Foot turn to Razor Blade and say. ' Listen to them two Indian how they arguing about we creole calypso. I never see that in my born days!'

Rahamut say, 'Man, I is a creolise Trinidadian, *oui*'

Razor Blade say, ' All right, joke is joke, but all you think it good? It really good?'

Rahamut want to say yes, it good, but he beating about the bush, he hemming and he hawing, he saying. ' Well it so-so,' and 'it not so bad,' and I hear a lot of worse ones.'

But the fellar who does help Rahamut, he getting on as if he mad, he only hitting Razor Blade and One Foot on the shoulder and saying how he never hear a calypso like that, how it sure to be all the Road March for next Carnival. He swinging his hands about in the air while he talking, and his hand hit Rahamut hand and Rahamut get a chook on his finger with a needle he was holding.

Well Rahamut put the finger in his mouth and start to suck it, and he turn round and start to abuse the other tailor fellar, saying why the arse you don't keep you tail quiet? Look you make me chook my hand with that blasted needle.

' Well what happen for that. You go dead because a needle chook you?' the fellar say.

Big argument start up; they forget talk about Razor Blade calypso and start to talk about how people does get blood poison from pin and needle chook.

Well it don't have anything to write down as far as the calypso concern. Razor Blade memorise the words and tune, and that is the case. Is so calypso born, cool cool, without any fuss. Is so all them big numbers like ' Yes, I Catch Him Last Night', and ' That Is A Thing I Can Do Anytime Anywhere', and ' Old Lady Your Bloomers Falling Down' born, right there behind Rahamut tailor shop.

After the big talk about pin and needle Rahamut and the fellar who does assist him went back to finish off a zootsuite that a fellar was going to call for in the evening.

Now Razor Blade want to ask One Foot to borrow him a shilling, but he don't know how to start, especially as he owe him already. So be begin to talk sweet, praising up the tune that One Foot invent for the calypso, saying he never hear a tune so sweet, that the melody smooth like sweet oil.

But as soon as he start to come like that, the old Foot begin to get cagey, and say, ' Oh God old man, don't mamaguile me.'

The Blade not so very fussy, because a solid meal in his belly. But same time he trying to guile One Foot into lending him a little thing, he get an idea. He begin to tell One Foot how he spend the morning how he ups the shoes from the shoemaker shop in Park Street, and how he eat big for nothing.

One Foot say, ' I bet you get in trouble, all-you fellars does take some brave risk, *oui*.'

Razor say, ' Man, it easy as kissing hand, is only because you have one foot and can't run fast, that's why you talking so.'

Foot say, ' No jokes about my one foot.'

Razor say, ' But listen man, you too stupid again! You and me could work up a good scheme to get some money. If you tiefing, you might as well tief big.'

' Is you is the tief, not me.'

' But listen man Foot,' the Blade gone down low in voice, ' I go do everything, all I want you to do is to keep watchman for me, to see if anybody coming.'

' What is the scheme you have?'

To tell the truth, the old Blade ain't have nothing cut and dry in the old brain; all he thinking is that he go make a big tief somewhere where have money. He scratch his head and pull his ears like he did see Spencer Tracy do in a picture, and he say, 'What about the Roxy Theatre down St James?'

Same time he talking, he feeling excitement in his body, like if waves going up and coming down, and he hold on to One Foot hand.

The Foot say, ' Well yes, the day reach when you really catching you royal. I never thought I would see the time when my good friend Razor Blade turn tief. Man, you sure to get catch. Why you don't try for a work somewhere until the calypso season start up?'

I tired try to get work. It ain't have work noway.'

' Well you ain't no tief. You sure to get catch, I tell you.

' But man look how I get away with the shoes and the meal! I tell you all you have to do is play boldface, and you could commit murder and get away free.'

The Foot start to hum an old calypso.

If a man have money to-day...

He could commit murder and get away free

And live in the Governor's company...

The Blade begin to get vex. ' So you don't like the idea? You think I can't get away with it?'

' You ain't have no practice. You is a novice. Crime does not pay.'

' You is a damn coward!'

' Us calypsonians have to keep we dignity.'

' You go to hell! If you won't help me I go do it by myself, you go see! And I not tiefing small, I tiefing big! If I going down the river, I making sure is for plenty money, and not for no smalltime job.'

' Well papa don't say I ain't tell you you looking for trouble.'

' Man Foot, the trouble with you is you only have one foot so you can't think like me.'

The Foot get hot. He say, ' Listen, I tell you already no jokes about my one foot, you hear? I ain't taking no jokes about that. Curse my mother, curse my father, but don't tell me nothing about my foot.'

The Blade relent. ' I sorry Foot, I know you don't like nobody to give you jokes.'

Same time Rahamut call out and ask why they keeping so much noise, if they think they in the fishmarket. So they finish the talk. Razor Blade tell One Foot he would see him later, and One Foot say, ' Righto boy, don't forget the words for the song. And I warning you for the last time to keep out of trouble.'

But the minute he leave the tailor shop Razor Blade only thinking how easy it go be to pull off this big deal. He alone would do it without any gun, too besides. He go only tie a handerkerchief over his face, wait until he get a chance when the ticket seller counting the money, and he go stick his finger in his pocket as if is a gun (one time he did see Alan Ladd do that in a picture) and say, ' If you don't give me all that money I kill you here to-day!' And afterwards he could take a brisk trip to Barbados, or British Guiana (he might even go to the States) and lay low until things cool off.

Imagine the Foot saying he is a novice! All you need is brassface; play brazen; do as if you is a saint, as if you still have your mother innocent features, and if anybody ask you anything lift up your eyebrows and throw you hands up in the air and say, ' Oh Lord, who *me*?'

He find himself quite round by Queen's Park Savannah walking and thinking. And he see an old woman selling oranges. The woman as if she sleeping in the heat, she propping up she chin with one hand, and she head bend down. Few people passing. Razor Blade size up the situation in one glance. He mad to bounce an orange from the tray, just to show that he could do it and get away. Just pass up neat - don't even look down at the tray - and just lift one up easy as you walking, and put it in you pocket. He wish One Foot was there to see how easy it was to do.

But he hardly put the orange in his pocket when the old woman jump up and start to make one set of noise, bawling out, ' Tief, tief! Look a man tief a orange from me! Help! Hold 'im! Don't let 'im get away!'

And is as if that bawling start the pliers working on him right away; he forget everything he was thinking, and he start to make races across the savannah.

He look back and he see three fellars chasing him. And is just as if he can't feel nothing at all, as if he not running, as if he standing up on one spot. The only thing is the pliers going clip clip, and he gasping oh God, oh God.

WILSON HARRIS

On The Cross-Roads

This is but a short note in appreciation of Samuel Selvon's achievement as an imaginative writer. Few writers in the West Indies are as loved and regarded as he is by the common people for his humane and creative spirit.

I first read Selvon's *Calypsonian* in 1960 in Andrew Salkey's anthology *West Indian Stories* (Faber and Faber, 1960). The depiction of Razor Blade, the Calypsonian, is haunting and memorable. He arrives on the cross-roads of Trinidad society at a time of acute crisis. 'It look like if work scarce like gold, and is six months now he ain't working'.

One of the archetypal figures associated with the cross-roads of the Caribbean imagination is Legba of Haiti. Legba is a lame god yet regarded as immensely strong. As with lame gods, or wounded figures of legend, whom we may perceive at times in ancient and modern theatres of the the imagination Legba is a seer. Hephaestus - another lame god - was regarded as a matchless seer on Mount Olympus of ancient Greece. The contradistinction between strength and lameness endows Legba with a peculiar nuclearity. He is consumed inwardly and the tension of elements within him immerses him in a fabric shot through with a numinous dividing line between self-destruction and self-creation.

Razor Blade's correspondence with Legba may seem far-fetched at first sight. Selvon himself perhaps did not contemplate this. But the intuitive links in reality seem profoundly true to me. Intuition tends often to be a misunderstood term. In depth 'intuition' serves as a hard-won key to open new dimensions of understanding and to break a frame or prisonhouse of convention. 'Intuition' therefore is part and parcel of an enduring quest and curiosity and labour and activity of the heart and mind and senses.

Razor Blade is imbued with depth. He comes to a shoe-maker's shop. He contemplates the table at which the shoe-maker works. The shoe-maker slices into the wood of the table at times as if he is blind to the leather upon which he works. The involuntary blend of wood and leather provides an indirect *sculptural* clue to a pattern of imageries that now ensues. Razor Blade steals a shoe when the shoe-maker retires into his shop for a moment. Rain is falling on the pavement outside of the shop. He keeps an eye on straggling passers-by on the pavement. His watchful eye identifies with them and would appear to achieve a synaesthetic leap into their passing - apparently sculpted - bodies for he sees them as 'sheltering rain', he identifies with their rain-soaked appearance as if they were shelters of rain, *carven or sculpted* bodies internalizing the element of rain that is falling *within* them.

The imageries that Selvon employs are indirect in their linkage and proportion but they impress me as a synaesthetic when one weighs the nuclear image 'sheltering rain'. On one hand a reader, it seems to me, may become sensitive to Razor Blade's slicing *malaise*. On the other hand the rudiments of self-creation are active in depth. There is a further complication in that Razor Blade's companion is known as ONE FOOT. These and other inner/outer features bring a numinous coherence to Razor Blade's fragmented existence upon the cross-roads of Trinidad society.

I hope I have succeeded in addressing the unusual talent at work in Selvon's craft, his comedy, his versatility.

A personal word. My wife and I met Sam at several conferences and we liked him enormously. He possessed a true gentleness of disposition combined with a sharp sense of humour.

GRACE ECHE OKEREKE

Samuel Selvon's Evolution From *A Brighter Sun* to *Turn Again Tiger*: An Expansion of Vision and a Development of Form

The terms 'vision' and 'form' are central in this topic, and so it is appropriate to start the discussion with a brief working definition of both terms. A writer's vision is the hope he envisages for his society deduced from his particular interpretation of the life and people that make up the world of his novel. Form, on the other hand, deals with the writer's manner of handling his preoccupations in his work; it is the stylistic choices he makes, to more effectively communicate his views about society and project his vision of that society. Before addressing myself to the issue that constitutes the major concern of this paper, I will briefly place Samuel Selvon in the context of West Indian history and literature, as this is relevant to his preoccupations in *A Brighter Sun* and *Turn Again Tiger*.

The history of the West Indies has been characterized by a lot of violence and trauma, consequent upon colonization and latifondia which ensured the economic enrichment of the colonialists and the degradation of the slaves and indentured labourers. This has presented the West Indian as a victim, rather than a maker of history. Lamenting this lack of history and its attendant loss of identity which the British historian Anthony Froude orchestrates, V.S. Naipaul, a product of this battered West Indian society, writes: 'history is built on creation and achievement and nothing was created in the West Indies.'[1] This negative conception of history in the West Indies posed a challenge that generated various creative solutions to the problem by West Indian writers. Each writer refused to condemn the West Indies to historical oblivion by addressing himself, in his own unique way, to the problem, and by successfully depicting the West Indian man as a unique creator of history in his own right. Written in the post-emancipation period of the 1950s, *A Brighter Sun* and *Turn Again Tiger* are, like Reid's, Lamming's and Harris's novels, Selvon's response to the problem of the Caribbean man and his history. These novelists have variously delineated the Caribbean man as having accepted and transcended the traumas of history, and as having gone on to create a place for himself in a new West Indian society, while not losing touch with his roots.

In an attempt to contend with this problem of displacement and its consequences on the Caribbean man, Selvon has projected a vision of growth for both the individual and his society in the two novels under study. The idea of growth in man can be perceived at various levels - at the physical, mental, intellectual, moral, and psychological levels. For the society growth can be social, political, economic, cultural, religious etc. Growth implies initial immaturity and naivety. In the process of growth, the individual graduates from his state of inexperience and immaturity, through years of exposure to the vicissitudes of life, to a state of maturity, experience, and awareness. The growth of individuals in a society reflects the growth of the society from an undeveloped, largely circumscribed society, to a civilized, sophisticated one acquired through contact with the outside world. This is the process of growth through which the Caribbean man, in the person of Tiger, and the Trinidadian society which is representative of the West Indian society, undergo in *A Brighter Sun* and *Turn Again Tiger.*

However Selvon's vision of growth in both novels is defined differently, and so too is the form in which it is explored. To better examine these differences and clearly show how Selvon's evolution from *A Brighter sun* to *Turn Again Tiger* represents both an expansion of vision and a development of form, I will examine Selvon's vision and form in both novels on a comparative basis. In *A Brighter Sun* Selvon shows Tiger, and symbolically the Caribbean man, as undergoing physical, social, mental, and intellectual growth. He grows from a state of innocence, naivety, and irresponsibility, to one of experience, awareness, and acceptance of responsibility that confers on him the mature status that is importantly lacking at the beginning of the novel. Selvon successfully presents this vision of Tiger and the Caribbean man, by carefully plotting his growth along various recognizable landmarks.

The first landmark in this graph of growth, is Tiger's marriage at the sugar estates of Chaguanas. At the beginning of the novel which opens at the individual level with Tiger's marriage, he is portrayed as a diffident, naive individual, still very much a boy, who has things done for him in which he has no say. His father arranges his marriage for him and he is so baffled by what is going on that he needs an old experienced man to enlighten him on what marriage is all about and what is expected of him as a man. Overnight Tiger changes from a boy to a man and his life changes from the carefree routine of 'days in the fields, evenings playing with other children, roti and aloo in the night' [2] to a life burdened by responsibilities with a wife to support, a house and a garden to maintain, and a duty to 'haveam plenty boy chile...[and] live good' as Ramlal tells him. Tiger is equipped with only a cow, a hut and two hundred dollars in cash with which to face life in Barataria. He has to grow into a man, all through his own effort, without the guiding voices of his past society, without parental direction. Thus, Selvon presents Tiger as full of uncertainties and doubts on his arrival at Barataria. It is significant that Selvon sets *A Brighter Sun* in Barataria, a fluid suburban community. Though he is mainly preoccupied with Tiger's growth, Selvon traces this growth through the interaction of both the Tigers and the negro couple, the Martins. To more effectively show the usefulness of a neutral ground like Barataria for the growth of a new Caribbean man, Selvon painstakingly establishes the past of, not only the Tigers, but also that of the Martins, to show how both couples have been shaped by their various pasts. Whereas Tiger's and Urmilla's past strikes us by its innocence and naivety, shaped by the largely homogeneous East Indian community in the sugar estates of Chaguanas, Joe and Rita Martins are products of a battered slum world where violence, brutality, prostitution, and bad language are the norm.

Selvon plots Tiger's growth to manhood in the context of such a society where people from such varied backgrounds with contradictory values, can sever themselves from the past and relate in a new environment shaped by new values. Thus, the Tigers and the Martins forge a new relationship in Barataria that rises above racial considerations. Tiger rejects his father's attempt to import the circumscribed Indian world into Barataria by advising him and Urmilla to '...look for Indian friend...Indian must keep together' (p.47). Tiger questions this advice, reasoning that a man's worth is in his humanity not the colour of his skin or the texture of his hair: 'Why I should only look for Indian friend? What wrong with Joe and Rita? ... Ain't a man is a man, don't mind if he skin not white, or if he hair curl?' (p.48). This liberation from the shackles of tradition and racialism expressed by Tiger, holds out new hope for the West Indian, and suggests the possibility of creating a new creolized society, in which there are no race and colour differences and no inhibitions or barriers.

In his early days in Barataria, as Tiger grapples with the problems of growing up, he naively perceives manhood as residing in the ability to consummate his marriage, to smoke, and drink rum like other men Tiger strives painfully to establish his manhood to his wife and others in this regard, and is constantly baffled by his failure to impress them:

> He wished that he knew more about everything - about planting crops at the right times, about living with a wife, and exactly how to go about the thing. In some way he sensed that unless he did it he would never cease to be a boy, to be treated like a boy (p.15).

As time goes on, Tiger establishes a spiritual affinity with the land which he cultivates and from which he earns a living.

Having contended with the responsibilities of a husband and a farmer,

Tiger takes another step up the ladder of growth. Urmilla is now pregnant and, as a prospective father, Tiger prays for a male child for as Ramlal tells him 'girl chile no good, only bring trouble on you head' (p.7). But when, contrary to his fervent prayers, the child turns out to be a girl, Tiger's reaction shows that he is still very much immature. He is disappointed and, in his selfishness, fails to consider his wife and child. Rather, he seeks solitude and restoration in the land, and wonders if worry is part of growing up. However, Tiger reconciles himself to the fact of having a baby girl and returns to his family, thereby accepting the fact that one does not always get what one wants in life, even if one has prayed to God about it. Despite his social and marital accomplishments, Tiger still feels inadequate - a fact which he contemplates thus '... To my wife, I man when I sleep with she. To bap, I man if I drink rum. But to me, I no man yet' (p.45).

As Tiger continues to grope towards manhood, he becomes more conscious of the outer world. He does not feel satisfied with his self-assertion in the smaller world of his home and his social extension in Barataria, neither does he feel complacement in his identification with the land. His mind begins to send out sensitive feelers that make him pose existential questions about nature and his environment, about man and life, about God and his own place in the scheme of things.

Selvon effectively contrasts Tiger's desire for self-expansion, to the complacency and unambitious life of his associates and friends in Barataria. There is Tall boy, the Chinese shopkeeper, whose world is limited to keeping his business thriving and his wife bearing children every year. There is Sookdeo, the old Indian, whose sole ambition in life is to have enough money to buy a steady supply of rum. There is the carefree Boysie whose only concern is to save enough money to migrate to England or America. And there is Joe who is satisfied with the day to day existence that life has to offer. They all see Tiger as over-ambitious.

As Tiger strives to widen his horizon and acquire more knowledge, life becomes more complicated and confusing. Overwhelmed by his ignorance and his increasing responsibilities as a man, Tiger becomes nostalgic for the easy, uncomplicated, routine life of the canefields of Chaguanas. These frequent flights into the sheltered world of his past, however, offer no solace, for a return will mean accepting defeat, wallowing in perpetual ignorance, and accepting the limitations of the plantation society - a situation which is the basis of all the confusion and embarrassment he is undergoing. Tiger's preoccupation with his problems alienates him from those closest to him - his wife and child whom he blames for his dissatisfaction with life. In his growing desire to know, Tiger sees illiteracy as another hurdle that must be cleared in his path to progress and growth. He envies Sookdeo and little Henry who can read and write. At he end of these questionings and confused gropings, Tiger however finds temporary solace in the land and his crops: 'And when the seeds burst and the shoots peeped at the sun, he felt that at least he could make things grow, if even he didn't have any knowledge' (p.82).

Another stage in Tiger's growth is when he graduates from the questioning stage and takes practical steps to acquire knowledge and widen his intellectual horizon. The first attempt is when he visits the city with Boysie. On this first visit, Tiger learns more about the city than Boysie ever does, through his exposure and his inquisitive nature. He experiences first-hand the topsy-turvy, impersonal world of the city where people work for their own selfish interests, showing little consideration for others, and where the colour of one's skin determines the treatment one gets. He discovers that it is not all beauty and respectability in the city as he had assumed.

As he becomes more fascinated with education, Tiger feels it will answer all his questions about life and the universe. Unlike Sookdeo who can only read the newspaper, Tiger has big plans concerning his literacy. But he finds out soon enough that literacy does not automatically confer maturity on a man, neither does it provide all the answers.

The coming of the Americans and the building of the new road mark a climax in Tiger's growth to self-awareness. Having learnt to read and having grown tired of the land and the routine of daily life, Tiger is poised for the progress and change which the Americans and the road symbolize. The people have to quit the land showing that they have graduated from the stage of an agrarian community. This marks the end of a way of life and the beginning of another. They have to exploit the social and economic advantages the association with the Americans has to offer. It is only people like Sookdeo, who are so deeply rooted in the old order of things, that will not survive the sudden and drastic change. But to Tiger, who is young and ambitious, it is a welcome change that holds out unlimited opportunities for self-betterment. Sookdeo's death makes Tiger take a critical look at his life and contemplate the prospect of death. He resolves to plan for the future and save money. Tiger questions God about the cause of death and rationalizes that '...everything have to dead when it get old' (p.156).

Tiger buys a book on road construction and gets a job with the Americans. As he learns more and gains a new feeling of importance and confidence, he distances his wife and child; communication breaks down between him and Urmilla who is afraid to tell him of her pregnancy. When eventually she does Tiger pours out his frustrations on Urmilla, even accusing her of infidelity. Selvon portrays the education and knowledge Tiger has acquired as destructive of happiness. It is ironical that while seeking the big things of life, Tiger neglects his basic domestic responsibilities to his wife and child. Tiger's association with the alien powers and forces of change precipitates a crisis in him which threatens to destroy his marriage and the relationship he has so painstakingly built with the Martins. This happens when Tiger decides to bring his American bosses home to dinner, a rash action which ends in his drunken beating of the pregnant Urmilla and the alienation of the Martins.

Despite the attainment of his aspirations - he has been promoted at his job and is financially well off -Tiger moves about in a restless, discontented state. Urmilla is sick; he loses interest in the road, and the wealth he has accumulated means little to him. His discontent is precipitated by the refusal of the Indian and creole doctors to attend to his sick wife in the night. In an angry outburst he declares with finality: 'Black people cud never rise in dis world' (p.18). The promptness with which the white doctor attends to his wife and his refusal to charge extra money, further convinces Tiger that a man's worth is not in his race, but in his personality. Tiger discovers again that wealth and success do not automatically guarantee satisfaction and happiness. Urmilla's stillbirth is the price Tiger has to pay for his sterile quest for importance and wealth.

It is a mature Tiger, who has come a long way and learnt the hard way, who tells Joe 'a man should hold on to what he have...the main thing is to be happy, nothing else don't matter as long as you happy' (p.194). It is the words of a man who has survived crisis after crisis and has grasped the realities of life, and so symbolizes Tiger's growth and maturity which contrast with his previous boyish impatience. His self realization also leads to a sound interpretation of human nature - it is based not on skin colour, but on the inner self '...they have good and bad all about don't matter if you white or black' (p.195). Thus, Tiger's creolization transcends the confines of colour and tribe. This is translated in his political vision of fighting for rights not only for Indians but for everybody.

Tiger, wiser with experience, tells Urmilla: 'You don't start over things in life,...you just have to go on from where you stop. It not as if you born all over again. Is the same life' (p.209). By the end of *A Brighter Sun*, Tiger has learnt a lot and has come to accept his responsibilities as a man. The new house he builds brick by brick with his own hands signifies this acceptance of the place in which history has placed him and the responsibilities it has conferred on him. Selvon is saying that the Caribbean man in the New World can never find satisfaction and fulfilment in escape. Rather, he must'reconcile himself to his place in society, and root himself in the land making the best he can out of it. Instead of envying Boysie who is preparing to migrate to America, Tiger in an unperturbed superior manner asks him: 'How you want me to leave my wife and child and house and go away just so?' (p.213). He goes on to tell Boysie, like an experienced adult instructing an impatient child, 'it ain't always a man does be able to do the things he want to do.' (p.213). This is a different Tiger from the impatient young man of the early days in

Barataria who saw his wife and child as impediments to his progress.

Though Tiger's journey to manhood and self-awareness has been a rigorous and rugged one full of obstacles and puzzles, the experience he has acquired is worth it. At the end of *A Brighter Sun*, Tiger laughs at the thought of returning to the canefields, showing the extent to which he feels liberated from his past. It is significant, however, that he still retains his hold on the land as is seen in his meaningful observation as he assesses the weather: 'Now is a good time to plant corn' (p.215).

As evidenced in the discussion so far, Selvon's major preoccupation in *A Brighter Sun* is to give a vision of growth for the Caribbean man, armed solely with his own inner resources as is symbolized in Tiger. As an individual, he has many choices at his disposal, and it depends on him whether to be a Tiger, a Boysie, a Joe, a Sookdeo or a Tall Boy. Selvon suggests that development away from the past and away from parental tutelage, requires applying oneself to one's responsibilities and becoming conscious of the larger world, as well as maintaining a hold on the land.

But in *Turn Again Tiger* which is a sequel to *A Brighter Sun* Selvon's preoccupations represent an expansion of vision. *In Turn Again Tiger* Selvon subtly questions the kind of vision he presents in *A Brighter Sun* . He re-examines his definition of the Caribbean man and his place in society. Selvon seems to cast doubt on the adequacy of the achievements of the Caribbean man in his new society - building a home, acquiring education and a greater sense of awareness and becoming an integral part of the new society, are not enough to make the Caribbean man whole; they are not enough to imbue him with a sense of fulfilment and complacency. Selvon is contending that, armed with literacy and awareness gained from his stay in Barataria, Tiger is now well equipped to appraise his situation and articulate his relationship with the past. It is only when this confrontation with the past has taken place that Tiger and, symbolically, the Caribbean man, will be fully liberated from the shackles of a traumatic past, whose psychological scars still lie buried beneath the veneer of civilization he has acquired.

Being a sequel to *A Brighter, Sun Turn Again Tiger* still has Tiger as its protagonist, and it is through the exploration of Tiger's return to the canefields of the past, that Selvon undertakes this redefinition of the Caribbean man. Selvon sets this return to the past in Five Rivers which is representative of the cane community with its usual social structure of white overseer and wife, Indian foreman, Chinese shopkeeper, and black and Indian labourers. Tiger is aware of the monotony of his life and his continued inadequacy, seen in his irresoluteness concerning his father's invitation to work with him on the cane-supervising job in Five Rivers. Through the purposeless get-together ('freeness') that Tiger's friends organize for him, Selvon shows the inadequacy of the Barataria ethic, and exposes a pointlessness in the lives of its inhabitants that justifies

Tiger's statement that '...a change always good, it make for progress...
You rotten if you stay one place all the time.'

The Tiger that we see at the beginning of *Turn Again Tiger* is a well-established, successful man by his society's standards. He accepts to go to Five Rivers only because he thinks his father, Babolal, is the supervisor of the cane project. To him, a return to the past with its distasteful memories of cane and all that it symbolized which he has come to hate and reject, is undesirable.

> He hated the cane. Cane had been the destiny of his father, and of his father's father. Cane had brought them all from the banks of the Ganges as indentured labourers to toil in the burning sun. And even when those days were over, most of them stayed shackled to the estates (p.1).

But Tiger is armed with the education and civilization he has acquired in Barataria. This not only makes him feel confident and distant, but earns him the respect and admiration of the labourers who look upon him as the elite that will teach their children and write to the government to improve the undeveloped community of Five River by providing amenities like good roads, good drinking water, electricity, schools etc.

But when Tiger learns of the presence of a white supervisor from Soylo and discovers this to be true, his self-confidence and aloofness are shaken. He finds himself in a dilemma - he cannot return to Barataria for this will invite ridicule from his friends. There is no escape; Tiger has to stay and confront this monstrous but concrete apparition from the past. As he inspects the white supervisor's luxurious residence, memories of the white supervisor lording it over his people in the canefields of Chaguanas rush through his mind. As Sandra Paquet rightly sums up, these are memories of '...defeated manhood, humiliations endured, exploitation suffered, his people victimized and abused because of their indentureship to the cane industry and the hierarchy of the estate village.'[4] This is the negative ethic that shaped Tiger's past in Chaguanas and '...he grew to link the rebelliousness with cane, and he had been happy to leave Chaguanas and go to live in Barataria, vowing never to return to such labour' (p.47).

But Tiger finds himself face to face with the very monstrosity he thinks he has successfully escaped from. As Tiger comes upon the white overseer's wife bathing naked in the river, the complexes of the slave mentality acquired from years of indentureship to cane which his years of freedom in Barataria have hidden, resurface. Despite his education and other achievements, Tiger succumbs to the age-old panic that his life in the canefields of Chaguanas has drummed into his head concerning the sacredness of the white woman, and he flees. Tiger regrets his panic and flight, but can do nothing to correct the dented image of subservience he has created in the white woman's sight:

He had run away like a little boy scared, because a white woman had called out to him. He, Tiger, who had his own house, who had a wife and a child, who worked with the Americans during the war, who drank rum with men and discussed big things like life and Death, who could read and write. Better if he had cringed, if he bowed and stooped and blurted out good morning like some ordinary illiterate labourer and asked if there was something he could do. But to run away, to panic as if the devil were at his heels - for that there was no forgiveness. (p.51).

Tiger's feeling of inadequacy and shame precipitates a crisis in his life. His inner turmoil manifests itself in his actions and social relationships - he becomes restless, alienates his family, drinks too much, and humiliates himself by undertaking demeaning jobs as yard boy for the white woman and literally placing himself at Doreen's beck and call. Doreen becomes the symbol of his humiliation and the degradation of his people. Tiger goes on to question the usefulness of education and the essence of reading lots of sophisticated books, when they cannot help him to solve the personal, daily problems he encounters in life. This disillusionment with education, makes Tiger burn all his books and give away his radio to Otto. Tiger symbolically strips himself of the trappings of civilization which are the symbols of his advancement, and this becomes a manifestation of the crisis going on inside him. Tiger goes further to shame himself by abandoning the ethics of civilized behaviour - he deliberately challenges Singh to a fight and everybody, including Soylo, perceives this negative change in Tiger.

It is Urmilla who, as his wife, is closest to him, that feels most the brunt of Tiger's selfishness and alienation. Her pent up bitterness is expressed in her chiding words to Tiger: 'You think you is the only one in the world growing up, that nothing happening to other people, only you' (p.126). Urmilla goes on to assert her presence and maturity which Tiger does not seem to be aware of. She too, like Tiger, has come a long way from a child-bride at the beginning of *A Brighter Sun*, to a mother and, in fact, the leader of the women's protest march against the men in *Turn Again Tiger*.

But this self-abasement points at Tiger's realization that psychologically he is still very much tied to the shackles of the cane estates which he had resented in his father and the other cane labourers. At least they make no pretence about their status like he does. This self-torture becomes the necessary psychological sickness which Tiger must experience to be able to successfully seek healing and regeneration and, finally, free himself from the complexes of a servile past and symbolically achieve wholeness.

Tiger resolves the crisis that has built up in him through the weeks by engaging in sex with Doreen. It is violent sex devoid of tenderness except for the urgency for self-restoration and freedom. With this sexual act, Tiger has symbolically vanquished the mystique of the white woman, and exorcised his inner turmoil and the degradation of his past. Tiger's bathing in the river is both a ritual cleansing of his body and an exorcism of the power of the white woman over him and his people.

Having emerged victorious in this crisis, Tiger achieves tranquility, and a full return to his hitherto neglected responsibilities to his family and the village. He is now truly mature and confident enough to assume the leadership role awaiting him in Barataria.

It is significant that Tiger abandons the job of bookkeeper preferring to participate fully in the cane harvesting at the end of the novel. He is now reconciled to his past and the complexes of cane, and so no longer has that debilitating hatred, which connotes fear, anytime he thinks of cane. At the end of *Turn Again Tiger*,Tiger finds that it has been worthwhile taking a step backward for now he has made two strides forward. At the end of the novel, Tiger significantly declares '...but is almost as if I didn't take no step backward, and it was forward all the time' (p.181).

From the discussion so far it is obvious that Selvon's evolution from *A Brighter Sun* to *Turn Again Tiger* represents an expansion of vision. The vision of growth that Selvon envisages for the Caribbean man and his society in *A Brighter Sun* though useful in creating a place for the Caribbean man in the New World, is limited and deficient in creating a truly liberated Caribbean man. It is in *Turn Again Tiger* that Selvon expands this vision by taking the Caribbean man back to the past of the sugar estate with its traumas, complexes, and psychological scars, to help him reconcile himself with his peasant roots by boldly confronting those destructive, claustrophobic forces from which he continually but unsuccessfully attempts to flee. It is when this confrontation has been made that the Caribbean man, like Tiger, will be truly liberated psychologically from the negative aspects of his history. And it is when this psychic wholeness has been attained, that the Caribbean man will be ripe enough to rise above his crippling position as a victim of history, and become a maker of history, as is symbolized by Tiger's elevation to a prospective political leader in the new Barataria community. He is now truly a man not only physically and mentally but, more importantly, psychologically, for it is his psyche, that has suffered from the indignities and complexes arising from indentureship to cane.

Selvon's evolution from *A Brighter Sun* to *Turn Again Tiger* also represents a development of form. The seriousness of vision and complexity of Selvon's preoccupations in his two novels, determine the form and stylistic choices he makes. *A Brighter Sun* exhibits a more simple and straightforward form than *Turn Again Tiger*. Apart from the constraints of a first novel, Selvon's vision of growth for the Caribbean man and the New World, demand a linear exploration of events and characters. Thus, Selvon's adoption of a linear chronological form in unfolding the stages of Tiger's growth, effectively serves his visionary purpose. As Tiger's consciousness expands and he learns more, so too the nature of his questions, the pattern of his thoughts and growth acquire more sophistication and complexity. The naivety and helplessness he exhibits at the beginning of the novel progress through a state of painful awareness of ignorance, to a state of knowledge and boldness symbolized by his loss of shyness and his fearless association with the Americans and the road (alien self-assertive forces), to the final state of tranquil acceptance of his destiny.

The characters are also explored along this linear chronological line. Selvon's major concern is to plot Tiger's growth from ignorance to self-awareness, and so he rightly dwells on the social, economic, mental and psychological experiences of Tiger. Other characters are also developed to an extent, but they are flashed in and out as they serve to illuminate and reinforce the character of the protagonist. Thus, the Martins are important in as much as they serve as a creolizing influence on the Tigers, and also as a comment on the process of growth of the inexperienced Tigers. Tall Boy, Sookdeo and Boysie all serve to highlight different aspects of Tiger's ambitions and growth to awareness. Even Urmilla who is growing up with Tiger, occupies a special place in the novel,for it is through her marital relationship with Tiger that the plotting of the whole cycle of Tiger's growth is made possible.

By juxtaposing the daily changes and occurrences in Trinidad with the vicissitudes of Tiger's life, Selvon is symbolically showing the symbiotic relationship that exists between society and the individual. It is the individuals and their collective experiences that construct the society. In the same way, as the society changes with the times socially, economically and politically, so the Caribbean man in the New World feels the need to venture out of the cocoon of the sugar estate, and expand his consciousness in a new fluid society. Significantly, Tiger's growth has not only been limited to the physical and intellectual aspects of life; it has also been extended to the material, because he has availed himself of the opportunities of his growing society. This is symbolized in his financial achievements in his road job and in his building his own house. By this act, Selvon is also contending that, though Tiger has expanded in all directions, he cannot afford to break away from the land. So, too, the New World cannot risk severing itself from the land that has nurtured it, in the quest for a link with the outer world.

From this, several images and symbols emerge as having been consciously employed by Selvon in *A Brighter Sun* to achieve his purposes. There is the image of land and crops. This image of growing things is constantly associated with Tiger throughout the novel. It is significant that each time he is baffled and overwhelmed by incidents in life, Tiger turns to the land and nature for reassurance and restoration. When Urmilla bears a baby girl instead of the expected 'boy chile', it is to his farm that Tiger flees to question the order of things, and finally reconcile himself to the reality of things. When he is embittered by his ignorance and inability to read and write, Tiger plants his crops and is consoled that '...at least he could make things grow, if even he didn't have any knowledge' (p.82). Tiger makes us feel temporarily that he is tired of the land and can do without it as the more fascinating road work with its promise of wealth and power consumes him, but at the end of his inner crisis, we see him not only building a brick house on the same site as his old hut, but also keeping a garden. It is symbolic that the process of building is couched in the image of a growing plant: 'Everything was past and gone, there was only the house to build now. To watch it grow, like a plant, brick by brick' (p.201). The prodigal, so to say, has returned to the land that engendered him. It is significant that Tiger finds inner peace and is able to mend his broken relationships, only when this return has been made. It is no surprise, then, that the novel ends with Tiger in harmony with nature, and at one with the land and the cycle of growth that is associated with it. 'Now is a good time to plant corn' [Tiger] muttered gazing up at the sky' (p.215).

Another symbol that need be mentioned, is the road which is symbolic both at the personal and societal levels. As Kenneth Ramchand has identified, the road is, an 'ambivalent symbol'.[5] On the one hand, it represents forces of change and progress socially, culturally, and economically. On the other hand, it is a destructive force which not only causes loss of life, but almost destroys Tiger's happiness. So, too, for the Caribbean society it represents both a progressive and a destructive force. Progressive in that it links undeveloped areas of the society with other more developed parts, as well as facilitates the movement of foreigners ensuring foreign influence on Trinidad. On the other hand, it can lead to a cultural violation of the Caribbean society. Selvon's achievements in language in *A Brighter Sun* are also impressive. He uses various shades of the Trinidadian dialect to delineate the various racial strains and sensibilities in the society. It is a truly creolized society. Selvon is careful to distinguish between his authorial English which is standard English, used in passages of direct authorial narration and description, from the creole dialects used by the various characters in conversations, discussions, and introspections. At first reading, this may appear heavy and cumbersome, but once one is used to it, the dialect flows smoothly, and even becomes fascinating and captivating.

In treatment of vision and form, Selvon's *A Brighter Sun* makes for easy and interesting reading. Tiger's growth is explored in a linear and straightforward manner; the language is functional, simple and fluid; the images and symbols are effective and easy to grasp; the descriptive passages are vivid and realistic showing Selvon as a writer with an eye for telling detail; and Selvon displays a sustaining sense of humour that runs through the novel.

Just as *Turn Again Tiger* represents an expansion of vision, so too it exhibits a development of form when compared to *A Brighter Sun*. Selvon's preoccupation with taking the Caribbean man back to the past history of indentureship to cane, is serious and is conceived in symbolical terms. Thus, though the story progresses with a definite sense of time and space, Tiger's experiences in Five Rivers are explored in appropriate suggestive images and symbols.

The relationships forged and characters portrayed are more complex and functional in depicting Selvon's concerns in the novel. Although Selvon is primarily concerned with Tiger's growth, he carefully plots the growth of each character showing how their lives intertwine with Tiger's The characters are part of the community of Five Rivers, each filling his own vacuum, but this does not diminish their individuality or importance. As Sandra Paquet has rightly identified, Selvon initially casts each character in the stereotypical mould, but deviates from this when convenient.[6] In fact, it is this ability to develop the character as an individual growing from certain expectations, to a new and unpredictable person, that marks Selvon's achievement in characterization in *Turn Again Tiger* . There is Urmilla who grows from the fearful, docile, Indian wife and mother, to a mature self-assertive woman who assumes a leadership role in her community. There is More Lazy who rises above the stereotype of the indolent day-dreamer, to a man struggling like others to work legitimately and earn a decent living. There is Otto who grows from the stereotype of the sleepy, indolent, insensitive shopkeeper, to a hard working man that asserts his manhood. There is Babolal who rises above the stereotype of the grovelling foreman, to a man of authority who commands Tiger's respect. There is also Soylo who grows from the stereotype of the sequestered old Indian detestful of human relationship, to a warmhearted person who has come to value Tiger's friendship. Selvon takes us into the past of each character, and shows us how this has influenced his outlook on life. This represents a more in-depth character study than is the case in *A Brighter Sun*, where characters like Deen, Tall Boy, Boysie, Sookdeo, are hazy creations with no concretely established backgrounds.

Selvon's artistic achievement in dramatizing Tiger's confrontation with his past is a mark of artistic maturity. Through images and symbols, this confrontation is made. The whole idea of the naked white woman and the negative associations she has for Tiger and the Caribbean society, is at the core of *Turn Again Tiger*. Thus, Tiger's past which his stay in Barataria has made him reject and hate, is personified in Doreen who becomes the concrete symbol of the indignities and complexes of the sugar estate. Tiger's initial reaction to this confrontation with the past is also communicated symbolically. As he flees from Doreen, his foot is entertwined by a horse-whip snake which becomes an image of the overseer's humiliating whip and an extended image of the white woman, the sight of whom is enough to rob a man of his confidence and manhood. The whole of Tiger's relationship with Doreen and the crisis that follows it, symbolize Tiger's defeat, his loss of

manhood, and his acceptance of the inferiority complex of his past. It is
no wonder, then, that the violent sex with Doreen becomes symbolic of
the exorcism of these complexes and the resultant attainment of peace
and wholeness. Even after the sex act, Tiger's bathing in the river is a
ritual cleansing of his body, and signifies the liberation of his psyche
from the fear of the white woman. Tiger's rebirth and regeneration are
communicated in the image of the snake changing skins, and that of
having walked through fire and emerging very much alive. Selvon writes
about the sex act:

> There was no pleasure in the memory for him - all the incident had done was to
> age him, afterwards he had shrugged like a snake changing skins. No triumph, no
> satisfaction, no extension of desire to make him want to do it again. Just relief, as
> if he had walked through fire and come out burnt a little, but still very much alive.
> (p.181).

The image of cane dominates the entire novel. The novel begins with the
planting of cane and ends with its harvest, showing the cycle of growth
that the characters undergo. Cane is of dual significance having
antithetic influences on the characters. At the beginning of the novel,
cane is an instrument of destruction which inflicts psychological
wounds on the characters, for it is the cane industry that made slavery
and migration imperative, and cane caused the indignities the labourers
suffered at the hands of the colonizers, and so is responsible for their
complexes and psychological scars. Thus, at the beginning of the novel,
Tiger hates cane and associates it with suppression and rebelliousness.
Soylo hates cane and associates it with the destruction of life, for as he
relates to Tiger, his son lost his life in a cane fire and his wife died from
the shock. Otto too has cause to despise cane, for it is there that his wife
cuckolded him with Singh, one of the Indian labourers.

As the novel progresses and ends, cane becomes an antidote with
therapeutic effects, and heals the various psychological wounds of the
characters restoring them to psychic wholeness. Tiger who, in the
opening page of the novel, establishes his rejection of cane and all it
represents by observing the canefields of Five Rivers from the distance of
a hill, not only descends into the valley of cane, but actively participates
in the cane harvest. This is only possible after his private war with cane,
during which he has had a face-to-face confrontation with and reconciliation to the traumas of indentureship to cane. This distance occasioned
by a hatred for cane, as is also seen in his bookkeeping job which does
not actually involve him with the cane, is closed when he relinquishes
his bookkeeping job to Soylo, and applies his energies to actual cane
cutting. This shows that Tiger has descended from the aloofness of his
education and creolization in Barataria, to a filial identification with his
peasant roots and the history of his people. Thus, the step backward that
Tiger has taken, has unquestionably resulted in two steps forward. At the

end of the novel, Tiger is, therefore, in a position to appraise the achievements of all the characters. His bitterness arising from his phobia for cane and what it represents, is lost. Tiger comes to respect even Babolal's confidence and authority in dealing with anything associated with cane, something which hitherto had been a vice in his sight.

Soylo too has been healed of his crippling hatred for cane, and the psychological scars it has inflicted on him. This is seen in his participation in the cane harvest as bookkeeper. Though he cannot go back to reconstruct his life to avoid the inevitable 'ifs', it is significant that Soylo accepts this, and reconciles himself to the tragedy which has almost destroyed his entire life.

Otto too asserts his manhood in the canefields during harvest by beating up Singh, his rival. It is significant that the deflation of his manhood and its restoration take place on the same canefield.

Even More Lazy is shown to redefine himself and his life style on the canefields. He leaves his indolence and dreamy life, and participates in the cane harvesting. It is significant that he moves from the feminine job of cane bundling, and assumes cane cutting - as a man he now deserves to drink with the other labourers in Otto's bar. It is even suggested that More Lazy may lose his love of indolence, and take up a permanent job.

Babolal, one of the most consistent characters in the novel, has proved himself in the context of cane, and, so, has deservedly gained permanent promotion to manage a larger cane estate in Chaguanas at the end of his present assignment in Five Rivers.

Urmilla who is fertile like the earth, is cast in the image of a fertility goddess - she 'was bearing a child, perhaps the greatest thing of all' (p.181). Her fecundity seems to be the all-embracing symbol that marks both the cycle of growth and harvest, and the growth of the various characters in the novel. It also marks the hope of the New World man and his society, now that he has reconciled himself to the past. In *Turn Again Tiger*, Selvon also distinguishes himself in his use of language Like Chinua Achebe in his historical African novels, *Things Fall Apart*, and *Arrow Of God* , Selvon successfully captures the peasant sensibilities of his characters through their language. He not only suits language to character, but also to environment. As Sandra Paquet has identified, Selvon roots his language in the calypso tradition of his people.[7]

Selvon's overall achievement in *Turn Again Tiger* shows a development of form seen in his artistic maturity. His vision is expanded, and is more wholesome and befitting of the new Caribbean man and the New World. This has also been explored through a more artistically mature and sophisticated form. The characters are more complex, and their lives crisscross in a common destiny defined by cane. The images and symbols are culled from the characters' environment, and have been effectively manipulated to communicate the novelist's vision for his society. The language of both the author and his characters are appropriate, and show Selvon as a sensitive artist who knows what is in character and what is not. All these are present in *A Brighter Sun*, but on a much smaller scale than *Turn Again Tiger*, For this reason, as has been substantiated in this paper, I would affirm that Selvon's evolution from *A Brighter Sun* to *Turn Again Tiger* represents both an expansion of vision and a development of form.

NOTES

1. V.S. Naipaul, *The Middle Passage* (London: Penguin, 1962), p.29.
2. Samuel Selvon, *A Brighter Sun* (London: Longman Drumbeat, 1979), p.6. (Subsequent page references are integrated into the paper and are to this edition).
3. Samuel Selvon, *Turn Again Tiger* (London: Heinemann, 1979), p.5. (Subsequent page references are integrated into the paper and are to this edition).
4. Samuel Selvon, Introduction to *Turn Again Tiger* , p.x.
5. Kenneth Ramchand, *An Introduction to West Indian Literature* (Middlesex: Thomas Nelson, 1976), p.70.
6. Sandra Paquet, Introduction to *Turn Again Tiger* , p.xxi.
7. Sandra Paquet, Introduction to *Turn Again Tiger*, p.xxi.

DAVID DABYDEEN

Passage from unpublished new novel, *The Counting House*
For Sam Selvon, with gratitude

'So what you bring me this time?' Kampta snarled as soon as Miriam approached the hut. It was past midnight, he had stayed awake to greet her, fretting and cursing all the six hours Gladstone delayed her. She was exhausted, she wanted to bathe and sleep, not engage with his anger, but he would not let her. He looked contemptuously upon the parcel of salted ham she handed over as if it were meagre booty. 'You mean you skin your back-end all night for a piece of ham?' he asked in mock disbelief, treating her with the same scorn he heaped upon her brothers when they returned from their nightly expeditions with only a pocketful of nails. He made them feel guilty for having betrayed him and their forebears. He had trained them physically, had tutored them with stories to provoke their sense of hurt and rage, and when the moment was perfect he released them on a raiding mission. But all they brought back were weak excuses. 'I don't care if Gladstone put two or twelve extra night-watchman to guard factory' he screamed at them, 'all-you just useless. When Gladstone land in Africa he raid enough to pack one hundred thousand shiploads, and all he had was one gun. You hear, one gun. And you know what else he had?' He threw the question at Thomas who looked away in shame. 'Brains. The man had brains. Brains is what most people carry in their heads but all-you head stuff with blood-cloth.' They fidgeted, the nails bulging in their pockets and digging into their flesh. They had walked the two miles from the factory in pain, but Kampta made them wait a little longer before allowing them to empty their pockets.

'Next time he open his coolie mouth at me I kill his rass' Thomas told his brothers when Kampta was far away. But he knew that it was an empty threat. He knew that Kampta was right to shout, for what was a shilling worth of nails compared to the money Gladstone was making from all of them.

'You have to thief and wreck and laze and fuck and drink and knock drum and make song that mock Gladstone, for soon your life done but *he* still own your legacy' Kampta had preached to them, 'remember your grandpappy them, black and angry though they weak with lash and two-three teeth only left in their mouth how they break the rest against sheep-bone and what-else bone whiteman feed them. Two-three teeth in their mouth like when goat enter cornfield and eat out corn and two-three ears only hanging from the husk. Is so whiteman eat out your grandpappy but even so, is rebellion they perform, and burn down canefield, and sharpen their teeth against whiteman, and sing Christian song in his ears till he surrender.'

Sleep. She wanted sleep, not fight, but he would not let her go.

'A piece of ham?' he repeated but still she did not answer. 'You mean the man heap up gold in his house but all you take is ham?'

'It come all the way from England' she offered, for want of something better to say.

'England? England?' he repeated quietly, turning his face to the darkness as if to better visualize the country. 'So you let him in return for a slice of England?' The quietness of his voice made her fear him. She could cope with him when he ranted or preached knowing that as long as she listened sympathetically his anger would subside. But she had also seen him talking to himself in a low voice as he paced the ruined garden - he had forbidden her brothers to plant, for planting was slavery - and she knew that he was pitchforking in his mind the nastiest of manure. He was frustrated. He had only an army of three boys at his disposal, insufficient for all the deeds of revenge his mind dreamt up. In such a mood she avoided him, making excuses to visit relatives in the neighbouring village which took her away for a whole day. But there was no escape now. Her thighs hurt from Gladstone's doing so even if she wanted to run away into the bush she could not. Best to look abject. Best to cry, to disarm him. Best to limp away, crying. In the morning, after a full night's rest, she could fight him. She could chase him from her yard for the hundredth time. She could taunt him for being a good-for-nothing abandoned coolie drowning in self-pity. She could order her brothers back to the garden. But now now. Not when he spoke quietly. She could feel tears gathering, not feigned, as she planned, but from real fear. With Gladstone she acted, squealing or weeping according to the role he chose for her. Sometimes she would confuse the masks of brazenness or terror so as to spoil his fantasies and leave him unfinished. But mostly she complied, for fear of her domestic wages which fed and clothed her brothers, with a portion put aside each week for her mother, when she returned finally to them.

'So everytime you lie with Gladstone, is England you lying with? When he heave on top of you is a whole country, great and heavy, pressing down on you so you can't escape?' He let the ham drop from his hands as if to free them for some deed. 'But Miriam girl, tell truth' he said playfully, almost with a small boy's innocence, 'you like England, no? When he put it in, you does close your eye and imagine you is whitelady riding through mist and meadow and all them other pictures paint on all the tin-cans he give you? You does open and close like how whitewoman does do her umbrella when the fine rain fall then sun come out?'

Is spit I get, not gentle rain and breeze, she wanted to answer, a middle-age man rising and falling and fanning me with his flab, and he so excited he fart and dribble, and by the time he finish my whole face wet with spit and the bed smelling of horse-manure. This is what I do for all-you ungrateful dogs, she wanted to say, and is my mother make me do it. When she come back she will want finery or else she will run away again...and if she run away again I burn the hut with Thomas and Joe and Peter sleeping in it, and I sprinkle white spirit over my head and light it, and I run through the canefield torching till I reach Gladstone's house, but if by that time the flame on my skin is low, then I go stoop and blow on my foot, blow steadfast till no breath left, till the flame start up and find fresh fuel underneath my skin and lick the whole of my body, then I stroll from room to room setting them a fire. Stoop and blow, and not make one noise, not one scream, like I stoop now quietly at your foot to pick up my ham, pick it up and dust it off, like I pick up myself from Gladstone bed and brush off the flakes of his skin. Like the preacherman break bread over my head and the white crumbs sprinkle in my hair and kindle and it become burning bush and I hear God denouncing me, *me*, from above, for sinning and how I must seek forgiveness. Like you standing over me now, raging with fire inside you which you want to put in me, purify me, and me kneeling as at church-altar but is not blessing I want but my fucking ham which I fuck for, roll in the dust for, so move your man-foot and fucking cock, you and God and Gladstone, and let me pass, she ordered but no word came from her mouth, only a sob which she dampened immediately for she would not cry real tears for him, not for any of them, not even for her mother.

Editor's Note

Most Australian children learn a poem by Mary Gilmore called 'Botany Bay'. It is a poem about our convict ancestors and the debt we owe them. I quote one stanza:

In old Botany Bay
Stiff in the joints with little to say
I am he who paved the way
That you may walk at your ease today

I discussed this poem on one occasion with David Dabydeen and he was quick to draw an analogy between old Botany Bay and Sam Selvon. For just as we Australians owe a debt to our convict ancestors so too do the younger generation of writers from the Caribbean e.g. John Agard (Listen Mr Oxford Don), Linton Kwesi Johnson (Sonny's Lettah from Prison) owe a debt to Sam Selvon for his injection of new blood into the English Language.It is a debt that David Dabydeen has always been quick and anxious to acknowledge. Dangaroo Press published David's first book, *Slave Song*. It was a book of poetry about the peasant canecutters of Guyana and written in Guyanese Creole. It was entered for the Commonwealth Poetry Prize and won it, the first book of poetry not written in so-called 'standard' English to win the prize.This was a tribute not only to David's ability as a poet but also to Sam Selvon, who took that first step.

Anna Rutherford

SAM SELVON

Sun

Will we ever discover tropic? Sun, insisting in the sky,
You make us wet with red dreams of freedom, burning
Whereas we will not burn. By what simple means
Your fire flames on these green islands,
To what purpose you there in sky we on earth
We cannot fathom. We squint back at you
In the canefield, slaving under your venomous fist,
We in streams bathe in your heated face,
And those who are a little wise ask
The old questions and watch the sky for rain. Sun,

Grinning on my shoulder, I with back bent
You with June's immortelle crawl in thick jungle
Deceiving with the promise of another day,
Priming my children for my death
And the catastrophe of their own lives. Knuckle
Of fire in my eye, yellow glare in air spinning
Over these green islands to attract people from the north,
Knowing as we turn earth how viciously we whisper
Comforting words to our neighbours to keep their chins up
Though their knees buckle at the nothingness of things.

(1949)

HENRY SWANZY

A Note on Sam Selvon

I can't remember when Sam started to contribute to *Caribbean Voices*, but it was just after the end of the War, when he was working on the Trinidad *Guardian*. I can just remember that it was a charming and unpretentious poem. 'Remember Harry's little car, And the vale with daisies.' Later it was about 'When the Yankees came to Trinidad, they had the girls all going mad.' He was one of the first West Indian writers to make contact with the BBC, when he came to England with George Lamming in 1950. Long afterwards, he came down to see me in Bishops Stortford when he spoke about the literary renaissance in the Caribbean to a local literary society. His contributions were mainly in prose, clear and unpretentious and marked by great accuracy of expression; over the years, I can still remember the sketches he wrote in verse and prose, such as his vision of the shore in Barbados, with the sea making the sky 'tremendously large'. Then there was the birthday broadcast that he and George Lamming made to celebrate the birthday of Frank Collymore, the editor of *Bim*. He was, however, not only a good writer but a great man. When he came to England, bringing his family, all of them fell ill with lung trouble, and had to go to a sanitorium at Pinewood in Berkshire, where I visited them - to find him quite undaunted. He overcame the temptation to abandon the struggle of making his name in London, among 'the lonely Londoners', but emerged to write for one of the leading English daily papers, *The Telegraph*, living only for a time on his savings. He also published a novel, *A Brighter Sun*, where the two main characters, the young Indian couple, Tiger and Urmilla, may well have been based on his own life. He was an admirable man, not least for his talent of silence. He never preached, but he fulfilled to the letter the words of Garcia Lorca on 'the coming of the black boy to announce to the gold-minded whites the beginning of the reign of the year of corn.'

JESSICA HUNTLEY

Nostalgic Moments

Long before I read the novels of Sam Selvon or even met him, his reputation as a young promising writer had reached a group of us in Guyana during the early 1950's. For this, we were grateful to Pansy Jeffrey and her late husband Jeff, who had returned to Guyana after living in London, England.

Sam, together with V.S. Naipaul, Andrew Salkey, George Lamming, and others, at the threshold of their career, were mainly writing short stories, plays and poetry for the Caribbean and World Service of the B.B.C.

The Jeffreys' had so stirred our interest that I looked forward to reading and meeting these writers. At that time I had no idea that I would find myself sailing for England soon to live among the very writers I so admired.

On my arrival, one of the first purchases I made was a copy of *Lonely Londoners*. I was fascinated by its humour and descriptions of living in London and wondered whether the writer had experienced some of what he was so ably describing. The copy of *Lonely Londoners* was passed around from friend to friend, read aloud to each other and took the place of a community newspaper.

Sam along with other writers gave of their time willingly and generously. The Kiskadee Cultural Centre, in North London, founded by my friend, Oscar Abrams, was the venue where they often read from their writings.

I had the opportunity of meeting Sam and his wife at a social gathering as the guest of Pat and Andrew Salkey. Sam seemed to have had the capacity of twisting the most serious discussion into something hilarious. He was, as we say, in his element, relaxed, as the humour of *Lonely Londoners* tripped off the pages onto Pat and Andrew's sitting room. During that evening Sam constantly called Andrew 'Trini'. This I found strange and could not understand. Everyone knew and accepted Andrew as Jamaican. Only years later it occurred to me that his humour consisted at times of turning things inside out. For Sam, the best compliment he was able to pay his friend and pasero was that of crediting him as being a fellow countryman.

One of the most memorable occasions was the opening of the Bogle

L'Ouverture Bookshop in 1975. Sam arrived late, in high spirits and in 'spirits'. He was anxious to read from his work and even though he stumbled over his words he nonetheless had the audience in peals of laughter. It proved difficult to get him to stop reading.

His departure from England to Canada left a void which was surely felt. Fortunately his regular visits to London, especially during the latter years, somehow made up for his absence. Not all of Sam's visits to London augured well. I recall a Forum on Caribbean Writers held at the Commonwwealth Institute. While Sam was reading from one of his works he was attacked by a member of the audience who was also a worker at the Institute. The ostensible reason for the assault was the reading by Sam of one of his early pieces which was considered sexist. Everyone was dumb-founded and shocked by the attack and to my dismay no apologies were publicly made to Sam. He did not retaliate as would have been his right. Instead he showed tremendous dignity and self control.

Another visit was the occasion in 1992, celebrating the writing career of his friend and fellow writer, Andrew Salkey. Sam's contribution was both hilarious and filled with generosity and modesty. He opened his remarks by promising, that since all the previous speakers had said so many good things about his friend, 'he was tempted to make a list of all the bad and negative things about him', much to the delight of the audience.

Sam recounted that it was not his custom to show his work to anyone and ask for their opinion. The one exception was when he asked Andrew to read excerpts from his manuscript *Moses Ascending*. Sam's contribution admitted that any success which he had achieved as a writer was in part due to the encouragement he received from persons like Andrew. At the same time the celebration was to acknowledge not only the writers but many others in and around the community who provided the warmth and humanity which made it possible for the writers to succeed.

He recalled...'the sixties and seventies were wonderful and exciting times. The success of one writer was the success of all. No one wanted to be the only writer from the Caribbean living in London...you wanted others to share in what was happening...it was a great feeling of warmth...'

SAM SELVON

Finding West Indian Identity in London (1988)

When I left Trinidad in 1950 I had been working as a journalist with the *Trinidad Guardian* for five years. During that time I started to write poems and short stories. The first payment I ever received for my writing was a cheque for two guineas from the *BBC's Caribbean Voices* programme produced by Henry Swanzy, which I treasured for months as a marvel before cashing it.

I was earning enough with the newspaper job to find myself being lulled into complacency and acceptance of the carefree and apathetic life around me. And that was the main reason why I decided to go to London, very much a young man, to seek my fortune.

I wrote to Henry Swanzy, who encouraged the move, and asked him to hold on to a payment of ten guineas the BBC owed me for a short story. I was hopeful that my little writing experience would help, but I was prepared to do anything to earn a living, and stilled my qualms with the thought that I could always return if I did not get one in London.

There was also a feeling for the English countryside and landscape which had possessed me from schoolday reading of the English poets. In the hot tropical atmosphere I dreamed of green fields and rolling downs, of purling streams and daffodils and tulips, thatched cottages and quiet pubs nestling in the valleys. And I wanted to see for myself the leafless trees covered with snow as depicted on Christmas postcards.

In my first English summer I went out to various villages and hamlets and felt the deep and exhilarating satisfaction I had hoped for walking in the fields and woods, which I had dared to dream about while reciting English verse under a mango tree in the schoolyard. It was one of the first things I wrote about. What I miss most about England after living there for almost thirty years is the peace and beauty and inspiration I found in the countryside: the land did not deceive me, as the people did.

My first lodging was the Balmoral Hotel in Kensington run by the British Council as a hostel for overseas students, but it also harboured a number of immigrants from the Caribbean, Africa, India, and other Commonwealth countries. It was my first experience of living among other West Indian islanders, happening in the heart of London

(handwritten margin note: the land did not deceive me, as the people did)

thousands of miles from our home territory, and I learned as much about them as I learned about the English, whose ignorance of black people shocked me. This was the country whose geography and history and literature I had been educated upon long before I knew that Port of Spain was the capital of Trinidad, so why did they ask questions like if the people lived in trees, are there many lions and tigers and elephants, and, of course, their amazement that I spoke English: How well you speak our language! Where did you learn? Once I edited a series of articles by a West Indian immigrant for a national newspaper, in which he said that his white workmates followed him around in the factory, even to the lavatory, to see if he had a tail! Years after it was commonplace to see West Indians working as bus drivers and conductors, the editor of the *Sunday Times* had to travel to work by bus for the first time, and professed amazement when his ticket was punched by a black man

The stories - the actualities - are manifest, but I'll only say this: not Buckingham Palace, not the West End or the Tower of London, or the glitter of Piccadilly Circus - not even white men performing menial labor as porters or roadsweepers, nor the fact that there were so many whites who could not read or write - struck me as forcibly, or rather impressionably, as this appalling ignorance about my part of the world, when I had been led to believe that I was coming to the fountainhead of knowledge. Though I was from a small island that might be flicked off the map like a speck of dirt from a jacket, I felt ten feet tall.

My first novel was written while I was working as a clerk with the Indian Embassy. (Even here there was flack - how could I be an Indian if I did not come from India...but eventually I got the job). What I didn't write in the office I wrote in the damp basement room in Bayswater that I was living in at the time. I typed the manuscript myself, on a small portable typewriter a friend had given me before I left Trinidad. I used the most expensive paper I could buy, a kind of thick parchment quite unsuitable for this purpose, but I thought it would impress some publisher. I showed the manuscript to Maurice Richardson, an English writer and critic who had befriended me. Three weeks later he phoned that he had found a publisher. My head spun. A naive Caribbean writer, I had just sat down and written about an aspect of Trinidad life as I remembered it, with no revisions, with no hesitation, without any knowledge of what a novel was, and bam! My first attempt was successful. When the publishers had me to lunch at a French restaurant in Knightsbridge I looked at the menu and forgot all the French I had been taught in Naparima College in Trinidad, except the word 'gateau', so I said I'd have that. But my native wit made me quickly agree when they thought I meant for dessert, and I airily allowed them to order the main course.

I lived in two worlds. Hanging about with Moses and the boys, and at the same time hustling to earn something with my writing, making contact with people in the newspaper and literary world. But more than anything else, my life in London taught me about the people from the Caribbean, and it was here that I found my manners. I was discovering a pride, a national pride, in being what I am, that I never felt at home. That was one of the things that immigration meant to me.

In 1953 I was hospitalised with pulmonary tuberculosis. When I came out the following year I decided to be a full-time writer, on the strength of a Guggenheim fellowship, which took me to America. It was while I was here that the idea of *The Lonely Londoners* came to me. When I got back to London I sat in a friend's house in Ladbroke Grove and wrote the novel there in six months. Two of those were spent wrestling with standard English to give expression to the West Indian experience: I made little headway until I experimented with the language as it is used by Caribbean people. I found a chord, it was like music, and I sat like a passenger in a bus and let the language do the writing.

The critical acclaim when the book was published is there for those who want to see it. Suffice to say that the language and the people added another foot to my ten feet, in spite of a few (inevitable) letters earnestly beseeching me to return to Africa.

It was always a struggle to survive in London, not only because of my non-whiteness, but money. Though I established myself there as a professional writer, I could never write fast enough to keep up with basic expenses like rent and food. The idea of full-time writing was a joke: I was cleaning bars or kitchens in the small hotels around Bayswater: when *Turn Again Tiger* appeared in 1958 I was swabbing out the shithouse at a small private club owned by an affluent Irishman in Paddington who said, 'I saw your picture in *The Observer* yesterday, I didn't know you were a writer.'

By the mid-70s most of the writers of the postwar efflorescence of Caribbean Literature had left London - England. I myself was growing restless. I had spent a great slice of my life inculcating English and European literature and culture, such as eating fish and chips and reading the *News of the World* every Sunday. As a growing boy in Trinidad, from the time of silent movies I was an avid fan because my brothers worked in a cinema and I could get in free. Whatever curiosity or cultural inclination I might have been developing was also due to American films. During recess at school we played cowboys and Indians, imitated American accents: I relate my youthful years with the American music of the 30s and 40s. (There are obvious reasons that the Caribbean has always come under American influences.) It was a part of my memory that needed experience to widen my concepts, and I was not ready to return to Trinidad, or any of the islands - it had to be somewhere on the Continental mainland.

It turned out to be Canada because that was where my wife wanted to go. She had visited relatives (who had immigrated there) a few times and glowed as she compared the standards of living.

We moved, lock stock and barrel. My native wit had thrown out a few feelers for my career as a writer; my name was not entirely unknown in Canada. But to tell the truth, it was almost like the time when I first left Trinidad, except that this was *real* immigration; selling the house, uprooting the family, turning my back on almost 30 years of life in London.

I have never thought of myself as an 'exile' - that word returned to vogue as people shuffled around the world getting settled after the war. I carried my little island with me, and far from assimilating another culture or manner I delved deeper into an understanding of my roots and myself. Immigrating did that for me, and provided the nourishment I could not find in the island to foster my creativity. I feel I do more for myself and my country by being abroad than I would have had the opportunity to do if I had stayed. I am, in a sense, still visiting abroad. But 'home is where you start from'. And should end from.

SAM SEVLON

The Leaf in the Wind (1952)

That September was one of many months, but the leaves, turning yellow and brown and golden on the trees and falling to be wind-driven on the pavements and swirled in the air, helped to urge me onwards. Waiting for something to happen, you never really know what it is, or what it will be. But one day birds in a tree chirp lustily and there you have it. Or a ray of forgotten sunshine falls across the desk in the office where you work.

Many days I saw them burning the brown leaves in the park. Raking them together in heaps and setting them on fire, and the smoke straight as a rod. The old man leaned against the rake and smoked a cigarette and watched the leaves burning. Old men always do that, when they burn leaves in autumn.

When the leaves began falling there was no stopping them. One day you saw a tree leafy and in the evening the branches were naked. The wind twisted and spun and lashed out at you: it waited around corners and outside doors. When it was behind you you didn't have to walk, and in front it braked you with sudden force, so you had to lean and step off again.

For some nights, pacing the streets, I found it bracing and invigorating, for though it was powerful it was not yet very cold, and when it swept you it left you feeling clean. I walked in it, groping for an intangibility to lead me out of the drear dampness I was in. I was indescribably lonely, lifeless and limp; I was a leaf in the wind.

I used to watch sometimes out of the office window at the overcast sky. I should have written much poetry - I felt like it, but all I did was scribble a line or two on the blotting pad, and the next morning I scratched the words off.

The quickness of darkness was a fascination to me. The way how, at four o'clock in the afternoon, a quiet dark would fall and lights go on in the mist and fog. It seemed there was never daylight; you got up in the morning and it was like night was still there, and you went out looking for the sun. If it ever came it was a sick, yellow orange at which you could stare unblinkingly, and you went through the day in a grey fog. Yet I remember moods when I thought it wonderful - I mean, you felt as if you didn't exist entirely, as if it were a half-life, a sort of dream, and you didn't want to go, not really.

All this while I kept reminding myself that it wouldn't do, that I had to get down to work, do something; but all I did was watch London and scribble phrases on the blotting pad. To make matters worse, I had reached a period where writing meant everything, a justification for living, and I exaggerated my frame of mind into a kind of fear for words. Once or twice I did make a half-hearted attempt, but I had no appetite. I just waited, waited for something to happen.

And then snow fell. I went out in it, turning up the collar of my coat. I went in the park and I scraped the snow off the ground and heaped it up. While I was doing that I thought it was a hell of a thing for me to be doing, but I went on all the same. There were a few children doing the same thing and hurling snowballs, and they must have thought me queer, a grown man scraping snow into little heaps, because the way I was doing it was kind of thoughtful, not as if I was enjoying myself.

One day I went to Kew Gardens to see amber and gold on the trees. It was beautiful. I soaked in it, and didn't make any effort to impose the picture on my mind, because I wanted that if I thought of it in the future, I would only remember hazily that it was beautiful, and not be able to recall any detail about a leaf or the shape of a branch. Sometimes when things happen to you, that's the way you like it to be, because sometimes when you think back about a thing too much or try to remember everything, you lose everything, and it might as well have not happened.

One night it was foggy and I went on Waterloo Bridge and I spat in the Thames. I watched the buildings and the neon lights. A man came up near me and rested his elbows on the parapet and watched too. He said it was a picture. He said he was a painter from Holland, and he was going to Ireland the next day. I said I was from the West Indies, and he said he loved our colours, that he had been to some of the islands. He invited me to his flat - there and then - to see some of his work. I have always had a fear - perhaps foolishly - of a spontaneous friendship with a male stranger, so I told him I was sorry, and went on looking at a barge part the water as it made headway.

My aimlessness was then three months old.

Christmas came. They were preparing for it in London since early October; there is such a lengthy build-up, every day you feel as if it's going to be tomorrow.

Nonetheless, I was determined to use the spirit as a sort of turning leaf in my mood. I joined a u-queue for my wages and afterwards some of the others said what about a drink, and I said, I'm for it.

I remember discovering then what I had been looking for, but the discovery was like covering one step in an unending series. However, that the leaf was turned was in itself something.

On a cold, dead night I walked into a cul-de-sac in Chelsea which they call World's End. It was my beginning.

VICTOR RAMRAJ

Eulogy for Sam Selvon

I was not surprised when some years ago I learnt that Sam, as a young man, before he turned to writing fiction, had wanted to become a philosopher. In all his works, even his lightest humorous sketches, and in his daily life with family and friends, we saw the philosopher in him. But he was not just any philosopher; he was a philosopher whose contemplation led him to look at the bright side of things, to see beauty and goodness and glory even in moments of deepest sadness; and this gave him a infinite capacity for resilience and optimism and good cheer.

I met Sam in person in 1971 and came to know him as a friend since 1978, when he and his family moved to Calgary. But I think I have known him since my teenage days in the Caribbean, when I began reading his novels, the first of which he published in 1952, when he was twenty-nine years old. Sam, as writer and friend, always has been for me and always will be remembered by me as the laughing philosopher, touched by the sad lot of humans but not overwhelmed by it.

Like Althea, Mike, Leslie, and Debra, like Shelley, Martin, Luke, and Sam, like his many relatives, friends, and colleagues, I feel a deep sense of loss at the passing of this warm and generous man. Yet I think that he would want us not to grieve his passing but to celebrate his life and remember the happy moments we shared with him: in my case, the endless hours of lively discussions of idly chatting, of playing Password and Scrabble; of figuring out cryptic crossword puzzles; of over-indulging in gourmet meals he delighted in preparing; and of visiting the Clubhouse at Stampede Park.

We shall all miss him in our own particular ways. I shall miss him when I stand in my garden and look at the green onions he planted one year. I shall miss him as I walk to the Faculty Club, picturing him beside me, hobbling slightly because of his arthritic knee. I shall miss him in the classroom when I am teaching his novels and shall no longer be able to promise that he will visit my class and talk to my students, who through the years have all responded to him with enthusiasm. I shall miss him on a summer day when I am out on Nose Hill Park and recall that we never did get a chance to walk there together as we often had planned.

But my sense of loss - like that of all of us here today - is assuaged by the belief that he is still with us, and if we should doubt that, we just have to turn to his books. I know that I shall always find him and he will always speak to me, as he does now in this closing passage from the story 'My Girl and the City'. In this story, written for Althea, thirty-eight years ago, in 1956, he portrays an old man in terms that make the perfect epitaph for himself:

> At last I think I know what it is all about. I move around in a world of words. Everything that happens is words. But pure expression is nothing. One must build on the things that happen...So now! weave! I say there was an old man on whose face wrinkles rivered, whose hands were shapeful with arthritis but when he spoke, oddly enough, his voice was young and gay.

SAM SELVON

'Galahad confronts the Colour Problem' - An extract from *The Lonely Londoners (1956)*

When that first London summer hit Galahad he begin to feel so cold that he had to get a overcoat. Moses laugh like hell. 'You thought you get away from the weather, eh?' he say. 'You warm in the winter and cold in the summer, eh? Well is my turn now to put on my light suit and cruise about.'

'I don't know why I hot in the winter and cold in the summer,' Galahad say, shivering.

But for all that, he getting on well in the city. He had a way, whenever he talking with the boys, he using the names of the places like they mean big romance, as if to say 'I was in Oxford Street' have more prestige than if he just say 'I was up the road.' And once he had a date with a frauline, and he make a big point of saying he was meeting she by Charing Cross, because just to say 'Charing Cross' have a lot of romance in it, he remember it had a song called 'Roseann of Charing Cross.' So this is how he getting on to Moses:

'I meeting that piece of skin tonight, you know.' And then, as if it not very important, 'She waiting for me by Charing Cross Station.'

Jesus Christ, when he say 'Charing Cross,' when he realise that is he, Sir Galahad, who going there, near that place that everybody in the world know about (it even have the name in the dictionary) he feel like a new man. It didn't matter about the woman he going to meet, just to say he was going there made him feel big and important, and even if he was just going to coast a lime, to stand up and watch the white people, still, it would have been something.

The same way with the big clock they have in Piccadilly Tube Station, what does tell the time of places all over the world. The time when he had a date with Daisy he tell her to meet him there.

'How you don't know where it is?' he say when she tell him she don't know where it is. 'Is a place that everybody know, everybody does have dates there, is a meeting place.'

Many nights he went there before he get to know how to move around the city, and see them fellars and girls waiting, looking at they wristwatch, watching the people coming up the escalator from the tube. You could tell that they waiting for somebody, the way how they getting on. Leaning up there, reading the *Evening News*, or smoking a cigarette, or walking round the circle looking at clothes in the glasscase, and every time people come up the escalator, they watching to see, and if the person not there, they relaxing to wait till the next tube come. All these people there, standing up waiting for somebody. And then you would see a sharp piece of skin come up the escalator, in a sharp coat, and she give the ticket collector she ticket and look around, and same time the fellar who waiting throw away his cigarette and you could see a happy look in his face, and the girl come and hold his arm and laugh, and he look at his wristwatch. Then the two of them walk up the steps and gone to the Circus, gone somewhere, to the theatre, or the cinema, or just to walk around and watch the big life in the Circus.

Lord, that is life for you, that is it. To meet a craft there, and take she out some place.

'What you think, Moses?' he asks Moses.

'Ah, in you I see myself, how I was when I was new to London. All of them places is like nothing to me now. Is like when you back home and you hear fellars talk about Times Square and Fifth Avenue, and Charing Cross and gay Paree. You say to yourself, "Lord, them places must be sharp." Then you get a chance and see them for yourself, and is like nothing.'

'You remember that picture *Waterloo Bridge*, with Robert Taylor? I went down by the bridge the other night, and stand up and watch the river.'

'Take it easy,' Moses say wearily.

But Galahad feel like a king living in London. The first time he take a craft out, he dress up good, for one of the first things he do after he get to work was to stock up with clothes like stupidness, as if to make up for all the hard times when he didn't have nice things to wear.

So this is Galahad dressing up for the date: he clean his shoes until they shine, then he put on a little more Cherry Blossom and give them an extra shine, until he could see his face in the leather. Next he put on a new pair of socks - nylon splice in the heel and the toe. He have to put on woollen underwear, though is summer. Then the shirt - a white Van Heusen. Which tie to wear? Galahad have so much tie that whenever he open the cupboard is only tie he seeing in front of him, and many times he just put out his hand and make a grab, and whichever one come he wear. But for this date he chooses one of those woollen ties that the bottom cut off. Before he put on trousers and jacket he comb his hair. That is a big operation for Galahad, because he grow the hair real long and bushy, and it like a clump of grass on the head. First, he wet the hair with some water, then he push his finger in the haircream jar and scoop out some. He rub the cream on his hands, then he rub his hands in his head. The only mirror in the room is a small one that Galahad have tie on the electric light cord, and the way he have it, it just a little bit higher than he is, so while he combing the grass he have to sort of look up and not forward. So this comb start going through the grass, stumbling across some big knot in Galahad hair, and water flying from the head as the comb make a pass, and Galahad concentrating on the physiognomy, his forehead wrinkled and he turning the head this way and that. Then afterwards he taking the brush and touching the hair like a tonsorial specialist, here and there, and when he finish, the hair comb well.

When Galahad put on trousers the seam could cut you, and the jacket fitting square on the shoulders. One thing with Galahad since he hit London, no foolishness about clothes: even Moses surprise at the change. Now if you bounce up Galahad one morning by the tube station when he coming from work, you won't believe is the same fellar you did see coasting in the park the evening before. He have on a old cap that was brown one time, but black now with grease and fingerprint, and a jacket that can't see worse days, and a corduroy trousers that would shame them ragandbone man. The shoes have big hole, like they laughing, and so Galahad fly out the tube station, his eyes red and bleary, and his body tired and bent up like a piece of wire, and he only stop to get a *Daily Express* by the station. For Galahad, like Moses, pick up a night work, because it have more money in it. He wasn't doing electrician, but with overtime he grossing about ten so why worry?So while other people going to work, Galahad coming from work. He does cross the road and go by the bakery and buy a hot bread to take home and eat. This time so, as he walking, he only studying sleep, and if a friend bawl out 'Aye Galahad!' he pass him straight because his mind groggy and tired.

But when you dressing, you dressing. Galahad tailor is a fellar in the Charing Cross Road that Moses put him on to and the tailor surprise that Galahad know all the smartest and latest cut. He couldn't palm off no slack work on the old Galahad at all. And one thing, Galahad not stinting on money for clothes, because he get enough tone when he land up in tropical and watchekong. Don't matter if the test tell him twenty guineas or thirty five pounds, Galahad know what he want, and he tell the fellar is all right, you go ahead, cut that jacket so and so, and don't forget I want a twenty-three bottom on the trousers.

And the crowning touch is a long silver chain hanging from the fob, and coming back into the side pocket.

So, cool as a lord, the old Galahad walking out to the road, with plastic raincoat hanging on the arm, and the eyes not missing one sharp craft that pass, bowing his head in a polite 'Good evening' and not giving a blast if they answer or not. This is London, this is life oh lord, to walk like a king with money in your pocket, not a worry in the world.

Is one of those summer evenings, when it look like night would never come, a magnificent evening, a powerful evening, rent finish paying, rations in the cupboard, twenty pounds in the bank, and a nice piece of skin waiting under the big clock in Piccadilly Tube Station. The sky blue, sun shining, the girls ain't have on no coats to hide the legs.

'Mummy, look at that black man!' A little child, holding on to the mother hand, look up at Sir Galahad.

'You musn't say that dear!' The mother chide the child.

But Galahad skin like rubber at this stage, he bend down and pat the child cheek, and the child cower and shrink and begin to cry.

'What a sweet child!' Galahad say, putting on the old English accent, 'What's your name?'

But the child mother uneasy as they stand up there on the pavement with so many white people around: if they was alone she might have talked a little, and ask Galahad what part of the world he come from, but instead she pull the child along and she look at Galahad and give a sickly sort of smile, and the old Galahad, knowing how it is, smile back and walk on.

If that episode did happen around the first time when he land up in London, oh Lord! he would have run to the boys, telling them he have big ballad. But at this stage Galahad like duck back when rail fall - everything running off. Though it used to have times when he lay down there on the bed in the basement room in the Water, and all the experiences like that come to him, and he say 'Lord, what it is we people do in this world that we have to suffer so? What it is we want that the white people and them find it so hard to give? A little work, a little food, a little place to sleep. We not asking for the sun, or the moon. We only want to get by, we don't even want to get on.' And Galahad would take his hand from under the blanket, as he lay there studying how the night before he was in the lavatory and two different white fellars come in and say how these black bastards have the lavatory dirty, and they did not know that he was there, and when he come out they say hello mate have a cigarette. And Galahad watch the colour of his hand, and talk to it, saying, 'Colour, is you that causing all this, you know. Why the hell you can't be blue, or red or green, if you can't be white? You know is you that cause a lot of misery in the world. Is not me, you know, is you! I ain't do anything to infuriate the people and them, is you! Look at you so black and innocent, and this time so you causing misery all over the world!'

So Galahad talking to the colour Black, as if is a person, telling it that is not *he* who causing botheration in the place, but Black, who is a worthless thing for making trouble all about. 'Black, you see what you cause to happen yesterday? I went to look at that room that Ram tell me about in the Gate, and as soon as the landlady see you she say the room let already. She ain't even give me a chance to say good morning. Why the hell you can't change colour?'

Galahad get so interested in this theory about Black that he went to tell Moses. 'Is not we that the people don't like,' he tell Moses, 'is the colour Black.' But the day he went to Moses with this theory Moses was in a evil mood, because a new friend did just get in a thing with some white fellars by Praed Street, near Paddington Station. The friend was standing up there reading in the window about rooms to let and things to sell, and it had a notice saying Keep the Water White, and right there the friend start to get on ignorant (poor fellar, he was new in London) and want to get in big argument with the white people standing around.

So Moses tell Galahad, 'Take it easy, that is a sharp theory, why you don't write about it.'

Anyway all thought like that out of Galahad mind as he out on this summer evening, walking down the Bayswater Road on his way to the Circus. He go into the gardens, and begin to walk down to the Arch, seeing so much cat about the place, laying down on the grass, sitting and talking, all of them in pretty summer colours, the grass green, the sky blue, sun shining, flowers growing, the fountains spouting water, and Galahad Esquire strolling through all of this, three-four pounds in the pocket, sharp clothes on - lord oh lord - going to meet a first-class craft that waiting for him in the Circus. Once or twice, as he get a smile here and there, he mad to forget Daisy and try to make some headway in the park.

By the Arch, he meet one of the boys.

'Where you going,' the test say.

'Have a date man, going to pick up a little thing down the road.'

'Listen, listen here to the rarse this man talking, about how colonials shouldn't come to Brit'n, that the place overflowing with spades.'

'I ain't have time man, I late already.'

'Lend me ten shillings.'

'I can't make it now, come round tomorrow.'

'Oh God ease me up, man. A cup of char?'

Galahad give him a shilling and move away from the Arch, watching up at the clock on the Odeon although he have wristwatch. The clock saying halfpast seven and he have to meet Daisy at eight. He start to walk a little faster, but was five past when he find himself in the Circus.

Always, from the first time he went there to see Eros and the lights, that circus have a magnet for him, that circus represent life, that circus is the beginning and the ending of the world. Every time he go there, he have the same feeling like when he see it the first night, drink coca-cola, any time is guinness time, bovril and the fireworks, a million flashing lights, gay laughter, the wide doors of theatres, the huge posters, everready batteries, rich people going into tall hotels, people going to the theatre, people sitting and standing and walking and talking and laughing and buses and cars and Galahad Esquire, in all this, standing there in the big city, in London. Oh Lord.

He went down the steps into the station, and Daisy was expecting him to come by tube so she watching the escalators, and he walk up behind her and he put his hands over she eyes, and that evening people in the tube station must be bawl to see black man so familiar with white girl. But Galahad feeling too good to bother about the loud tones in them people eyes. Tonight is his night. This was something he uses to dream about in Trinidad. The time when he was leaving, Frank tell him: 'Boy, it have bags of white pussy in London, and you will eat till you tired.' And now, the first date, in the heart of London, dressed to kill, ready to escort the number around the town, anywhere she want to go, any place at all.

Daisy was dress up plenty, she look different than when she in the plant with a pair of jeans and a overalls on. All the grease and dirt wash off the hands, the hair comb well, the dress is a sort of cotton but it have all sorts of coloured designs on it and it look pretty, and she have on lipstick for so. She look real sharp, and when he was coming up he notice the trim legs and the straight lines of the nylons, and the highheel shoes.

Daisy move his hands and say, 'Oh, it's you. I thought you were coming by tube.' And she look a little embarrass, but Galahad didn't notice.

'What time it is now in Trinidad?' Galahad look at the big clock, watching for Trinidad; the island so damn small it only have a dot and the name. 'That is where I come from,' he tell Daisy, 'you see how far it is from England?'

'We'll be late,' Daisy say.

'Which part you want to go,' Galahad ask,' 'anywhere at all. Tonight we on a big splurge.'

'They're showing *The Gladiator* at the Hippodrome, and I want to see it.'

'Pictures! Is pictures you want to go tonight?'

'Well it's Sunday and all the theatres are closed.'

'Who acting in *The Gladiator*?'

'Victor Mature.'

'Well if that is what you want, all right. But I was thinking we could go some place and have a good time, being as is the only night I have off for the whole week, and you too.'

So they went to this theatre that showing *The Gladiator*, and Galahad feeling good with this piece of skin walking with him. But when he look at prices to enter, he couldn't help saying how it was a lot of money, not that he mind, but he know that that same picture would come down in the Water and show for two and six.

'This is the West End,' Daisy reminds him.

'All right, even if is a pound we still going.'

After the picture they went to a restaurant and eat a big meal and Galahad buy a bottle of French wine, telling the waiter to bring the best.

The summer night descend with stars, they walking hand in hand, and Galahad feeling hearts.

'It was a lovely evening - ' Daisy began.

'Come and go in the yard,' Galahad say.

'What?' Daisy say.

'The yard. Where I living.'

All this time he was stalling, because he feeling a sort of shame to bring the girl in that old basement room, but if the date end in fiasco he know the boys would never finish giving him tone for spending all that money and not eating.

Daisy start to hesitate but he make haste and catch a number twelve, telling she that it all on the way home. When they hop off by the Water she was still getting on prim, but Galahad know was only grandcharge, and besides the old blood getting hot, so he walk Daisy brisk down the road, and she quiet as a mouse. They went down the basement steps and Galahad fumble for the key, and when he open the door a whiff of stale food and old clothes and dampness and dirt come out the door and he only waiting to hear what Daisy would say.

But she ain't saying nothing, and he walk through the passage and open the door and put the light on.

Daisy sit down on the bed and Galahad say:'You want a cup of char?' And without waiting for any answer he full the pot in the tap and put it on the ring and turn the gas on. He feel so excited that he had to light a cigarette, and he keep saying Take it easy to himself.

'Is this your room?' Daisy say, looking around and shifting about as if she restless.

'Yes,' Galahad say, 'You like it?'

'Yes,' Daisy say.

Galahad throw a copy of *Ebony* to her and she begin to turn the pages.

With all the excitement Galahad taking off the good clothes carefully and slowly, putting the jacket and trousers on the hanger right away, and folding up the shirt and putting it in the drawer.

When the water was boiling he went to the cupboard and take out a packet of tea, and he shake some down in the pot.

Daisy look at him as if he mad.

'Is that how you make tea?' she ask.

'Yes,' Galahad say, 'No foolishness about it. Tea is tea - you just drop some in the kettle. If you want it strong, you drop plenty. If you want it weak, you drop little bit. And so you make a lovely cuppa.'

He take the kettle off and rest it on a sheet of *Daily Express* on the ground. He bring two cups, a spoon, a bottle of milk and a packet of sugar.

'Fix up,' he say, handing Daisy a cup.

They sit down there sipping the tea and talking.

'You get that raise the foreman was promising you?' Galahad ask, for something to say.

'What did you say? You know it will take me some time to understand everything you say. The way you West Indians speak!'

'What wrong with it?' Galahad ask. 'Is English we speaking.'

And so he coasting a little oldtalk until the tea finish, and afterwards he start to make one set of love to Daisy .

'It was battle royal in that basement, man,' he tell Moses afterwards, and he went on to give a lot of detail, though all of that is nothing to a old veteran like Moses, is only to Galahad is new because is the first time with a white number. Moses smile a knowing smile, a tired smile, and 'Take it easy,' he tell Sir Galahad .

SAM SELVON

A Note on Dialect *(1971)*

As a writer who has used dialect with great success as a literary form I was surprised when the matter came up at one of the sessions and was flippantly dismissed by a new novelist from the Caribbean. My regret at not taking up the point then is not for my dialect work - which stands on its own merit and has been acclaimed in England and America - but that the students might have been misguided into a belief that the dialect is frivolous and has no lasting value: indeed, that it has none at all according to the remarks made. I think I can say without a trace of modesty that I was the first Caribbean writer to explore and employ dialect in a full-length novel where it was used in both narrative and dialogue. I was boldfaced enough to write a complete chapter in a stream-of-consciousness style (I think that's what it is called) without punctuation and seemingly disconnected, a style difficult enough for the average reader with 'straight' English.

It was *after* the success of this novel, *The Lonely Londoners* that I did several short stories in dialect, 'by request'. Later, after two 'straight' novels, *Turn Again Tiger* and *I Hear Thunder* I lambasted them with another dialect novel, *The Housing Lark*. By then critics and reviewers were not even bothered about the dialect - they were more concerned with the content of the book.

I feel that if an author has to explain his work he might as well not write. My dialect books and short stories have been written and assessed. That speaks for itself. Unfortunately some of them are out of print but I am hoping to have them re-issued.

This short note is not in defence of the use of dialect in writing - I don't think that's necessary at all. It is really a kind of apology to the Conference that I did not speak up at the time of the session and make rab.

A Note on the above

In Spring 1971 I organised at the University of Aarhus, Denmark, the first Commonwealth literature conference to be held in Europe. It was also at this conference that we formed the first branch of EACLALS and *Commonwealth Newsletter*, the predecessor of *Kunapipi*, came into being.

We followed the practice that had been established in Leeds in 1964 when the

Association was formed, namely to include both writers and critics. Classes in the English Department were cancelled and for a whole week writers and critics spoke to an audience of over two hundred people. Amongst the West Indian writers were Wilson Harris, Shiva Naipaul and in a paper called ' The Writer Without a Society' he expressed ideas very similar to those expressed by his brother V.S. Naipaul and as Sam says dialect was 'flippantly dismissed'. Sam did not reply at the time but when he heard that I was going to publish the papers he asked that the above piece be included and I readily agreed.

To add a personal note. Sam Selvon was a friend of mine for over thirty years and he remained at the end as I found him at the beginning, a warm, gentle, humorous, modest and humane man. In a tribute, Jeremy Taylor has written about how, during English lessons on long hot afternoons in Caribbean classrooms, his students reacted to Sam's work: 'Somehow Sam Selvon always managed to speak to those youngsters through all the boredom and the heat. Once we got into stories from *Ways of Sunlight* or another episode from *The Lonely Londoners*, they perked up, they were laughing, anxious...to read more...Those students were seeing *themselves* in a book: the way they spoke, the way they thought and laughed' [1] I have had the same experience with my students, particularly when teaching *A Brighter Sun*. Unlike Jeremy's students, mine were not seeing themselves but Sam had the ability to introduce them to his own rich world, to help them see and understand a world very different from their own. It was a funny, sad, bittersweet, natural world. It was a different world but it did what I believe Sam would have wanted it to do, it showed them that other cultures exist, that they were as rich as their own and in achieving these aims created a tolerance so much needed in our world today.

Anna Rutherford

1.   Jeremy Taylor, 'Play it Again Sam', *BIWI Flight Magazine* (Autumn, 1994), p.31.

ANNE WALMSLEY

Sam Selvon: Gifts

The Winter 1960 issue of the *Tamarack Review*, devoted to West Indian writing, opened with Sam Selvon's poem 'Sun' followed soon after by his story 'Come Back to Grenada'. I bought a copy at Sangsters in Harbour Street, Kingston, Jamaica, early in 1961; I'd already borrowed *Ways of Sunlight* published in 1957, from the Trelawny Public Library in Falmouth, near the school where I was teaching. Lines of the poem 'Sun' charged me then as they do today:

> Knuckle
> Of fire in my eye, yellow glaze in air spinning
> Over these green islands to attract people from the north.
> Knowing as we turn earth how viciously we whisper
> Comforting words to our neighbours to keep their chins up
> Though their knees buckle at the nothingness of things.

The story 'The Village Washer' in particular intrigued and excited the 13 and 14 years old Jamaican girls in my English classes. I included it in a selection of West Indian writing for a proposed school anthology shown to Longmans the following year - and it was the main reason for the book's rejection; the Jamaican Ministry of Education was against texts containing 'dialect'. In London, in the mid 1960s, I offered the selection to Longmans again, including the same Selvon story - and with a Selvon book title, *Caribbean Cascadura*, from that Trinidad legend cited in the first story of *Ways of Sunlight:* 'those who eat the cascadura will end their days in the island no matter where they wander.' Longmans now accepted the anthology, but not the title. My next suggestion, *The Sun's Eye*, from an A.J. Seymour poem, echoed Selvon's 'Sun'.

Selvon agreed to the inclusion of his story, with the sensible and farsighted proviso that a repeat fee be paid on each reprint of the anthology. His autobiographical note was printed exactly as he typed it: 'When I went to school in Trinidad, where I was born, we didn't have text-books like this one in those days...I didn't complete my education because things were brown and I had to hustle a work.' Then in the late 1960s, he rang me at Longmans where I was now Caribbean editor: might we be interested in republishing some of his early books? The enquiry was on Andrew Salkey's recommendation; Sam Selvon and I had not yet met, despite the Caribbean Artists Movement, of which he was, as he later explained, 'very much on the sidelines'. So it was that in 1971, 1972 and 1973 *A Brighter Sun, The Lonely Londoners* and *Ways of Sunlight* reappeared in their first Longman editions and began to reach an ever-growing new readership, in the Caribbean and in Britain. What a gift these books were to a publisher! Minimal risk and editorial overheads, with continuing rights to republish - to Longman's great benefit and not, I suspect, to the appropriate cumulative benefit of the author. And, as I now see, what untold gifts they brought to me! For those three reprints grounded our friendship and, inexplicably and undeservedly, Sam expressed generous thanks for them ever after. We met first at the Longman offices or in central London; most memorably, I went at least twice to the Selvons' home in Streatham - 36 Woodside Avenue - for one of Sam's fragrant curries with Althea and the young Michael, Leslie and Debra. All this could have been lost when Sam and his family emigrated to Canada in 1978 and I left Longmans. Amazingly, and thanks to Sam's letter-writing, the friendship deepened. His letters always gave me detailed family news: his delight, in 1984, that at last they had a family home in Calgary; his joy in 1985 at being able to take the whole family to Trinidad, joined there by his sister, Elsie, from London, for his Honorary Doctorate from UWI, when they all stayed with Ken Ramchand; his satisfaction at being writer-in-residence at Winnipeg University, tempered by its distance from home; and how a similar appointment at Calgary brought 'great relief and comfort to be so near the family.' His letters shared hopes and disappointments over his published books, and over his current writing. And Sam's letters always responded to my news, with concerned enquiries for my welfare. They acknowledged and nurtured our friendship: 'it's made me happy to write to you', 'you have warmed my morning with your letter - it is really strengthening to be assured of friendship.'

Sam Selvon's last letter to me was in July 1992, after he had taken part in Salkey's Score - the symposium and celebration around the work of Andrew Salkey. He wrote of 'the privilege to be in London to share the wonderful revival of a period of time in our history which marked the beginning of our *FUTURE*'. My book on the Caribbean Artists Movement had come out at the same time. 'What a painstaking and *loving* book you have written, stamping our literary and cultural history indelibly on the sands of time! Are you sure there are not a few drops of Caribbean blood running in your veins?' Sam, who had so little involvement in CAM, wrote the most precious letter about it, thanks to his generosity and his gift for friendship. When I last saw Sam - like so many of us in London - at the South Bank in late October 1993, he was just off to Trinidad, and I to Guyana. We shared each other's delight in the prospect of being back. While I mourn Sam Selvon's loss, I rejoice that he ended his days on the island, warmed by the presence of his family and strengthened by his friends. All the words he gave us - as a writer, as a friend, sing on and on.

SUSHIELA NASTA

Setting Up Home in a City of Words: Sam Selvon's London Novels

Wat a joyful news, Miss Mattie,
I feel like me heart gwine burs'
Jamaica people colonizin
Englan' in reverse
                    Louise Bennett, 'Colonisation in Reverse', *Jamaica Labrish* (1966)

No Barbadian, no Trinidadian, no St Lucian, no
islander from the West Indies sees himself as a
West Indian until he encounters another islander
in a foreign country.... In this sense most West
Indians of my generation were born in England...
                    George Lamming, *The Pleasures of Exile* (1960)

Although a sense of the need to migrate clearly affected early writers
born in the Caribbean such as the Jamaican, Claude McKay who left in
1912 for the United States, the period immediately following the Second
World War was particularly important for the arrival in London of a
number of talented young West Indians artists. London, as Henry
Swanzy the producer of the influential BBC Radio programme *Caribbean
Voices* once aptly observed, had become a 'literary headquarters'. It had
become a centre where writers from the various islands were meeting for
the first time and attempted paradoxically perhaps after departure from
the islands to establish a firm West Indian cultural identity. It was also a
time when over 40,000 West Indians emigrated to Britain in search of
employment. Originally invited to the 'mother-country' by the post-war
government as an attempt to solve the immediate labour crisis following
the Second World War and commonly known as the 'Windrush
generation', these islanders moved to Britain expectant to improve their
standard of living. But the streets of London were not paved with gold
and the journey from island to city, was in many cases one only of
disappointment and disillusion. Moses the eponomous 'hero' of Sam
Selvon's well-known group of novels on the immigrant experience in
Britain - *The Lonely Londoners* (1956), *Moses Ascending*(1975) and *Moses
Migrating*(1983) makes the following satiric observations on the plight of
black Londoners:

The alarms of all the black people in Brit'n are timed to ring before the rest of the population. It is their destiny to be up and about at the crack o'dawn. In these days of pollution and environment, he is very lucky, for he can breathe the freshest air of the new day before anybody else. He does not know how fortunate he is. He does not know how privileged he is to be in charge of the city whilst the rest of Brit'n is still abed. He strides the streets, he is Manager of all the offices in Threadneedle Street, he is Chief Executive of London Transport and British Railways, he is superintendent of all the hospitals,he is landlord of all the mansions in Park Lane and Hampstead....He ain't reach the stage yet of scrubbing the floors of Buckingham Palace ..... There is a scramble amongst the rest of the loyal population for these royal jobs, but with time, he too might be exalted to these ranks - who knows? Instead of moaning and groaning about his sorrows,he should stop and think and count these blessings reserved solely for him. He should realise that if it wasn't for him the city would go on sleeping forever.[1]

The black man is therefore the backbone of the city but we see him only at night.many fictional and non-fictional accounts document this period of West Indian cultural history. Whilst Selvon's pioneering work *The Lonely Londoners* was emblematic in its creation of a black colony in the heart of the city, there are many others such as George Lamming's *The Emigrants*(1954), as well as his well-known collection of non-fictional essays, The *Pleasures of Exile*(1960), Andrew Salkey's *Escape to an Autumn Pavement*(1963)and V.S.Naipaul's *The Mimic Men*(1967) which also deal with the loneliness and disillusion of the early immigrant experience.interestingly few women writers, apart from Jean Rhys whose work spanned the pre-war period, were published at this time largely due to the fact that the first wave of immigration to Britain was predominantly male. Other women writing during this period such as the poets, Una Marson or Louise Bennett, gained little recognition in the publishing world. And this imbalance between the sexes is often reflected in the subject-matter of these early works where there is a notable absence of successful love relationships, children or any organic family life.

Jean Rhys's *Voyage in the Dark*(1934) for instance portrays a familiar sense of dislocation and cultural confusion as Anna Morgan, her white Creole heroine, attempts to feel her way in an unwelcoming city. Her England is a world where no homes are experienced and Anna , like many of Rhys's later heroines, survives on the edges of the society in an almost surreal metropolis which is frequently reduced to nothing more than colourless rooms in sordid boarding-houses. The characters, like V.S.Naipaul's Ralph Singh in *The Mimic Men*(1967) or even the 'boys' in Selvon's *The Lonely Londoners* remain adrift whatever their situation:

It was as if a curtain had fallen, hiding everything I had ever known. It was almost like being born again. The colours were different, the smells different, the feeling things gave you right down inside yourself was different. Not just the difference between heat; light; darkness; grey. But a difference in the way I was frightened and the way I was happy...Sometimes it was as if I were back there and England were a dream. At other times England was the real thing and out there was the dream, but I could never fit them together.[2]

This early representation in Rhys of a kind of cultural schizophrenia points to several fundamental issues which are still major preoccupations in the works of many contemporary second-generation writers, writers who are giving voice to the experiences of their own generation, a generation often born in the United Kingdom but still without a clear sense of home either in Britain or back in the islands. Writers such as Caryl Phillips, Grace Nichols, Fred D'Aguiar, Joan Riley, Merle Collins, David Dabydeen and Linton Kwesi Johnson to name but a few all reflect a concern with these issues. For the experience of Britain does not create a simple antithesis between tropical exoticism and darkness in a cold clime, nor is the meeting of the two worlds in the imagination easily reduced to a nostalgic vision of a lost paradaisical childhood and an alien world to replace it. The problem is more centrally one of different ways of seeing, of different modes of apprehending reality which have to be comprehended within a new context. Even for Jean Rhys in the 1930's, (who is commonly categorised a white West Indian), the main difficulty was to come to terms with the idea of London as an illusion, as a dream built on the foundations of the colonial myth; a myth which has to be demythologized in the mind of the artist who comes from a previously colonized world.

Yet ironically, it was London that created the possibility, in many cases, of a bridge between the past - a history of racial admixture, cultural disorientation and economic exploitation - and the present, which posited a strong need to establish a West Indian 'cultural pedigree'. As Donald Hinds noted in *Journey to an Illusion* escape from the islands was frequently a stage on the route to self-discovery:

> Deep down I knew I loved my persecutors. Our Caribbean background was shaped by English things... but at last I was coming to terms with myself... I am indeed grateful to the English. Grateful for forgetting me in order to discover myself.[3]

The birth of a Caribbean consciousness by confrontation with the 'mother-country', and the re-definition created by the juxtaposition of the two worlds is a central theme in a great deal of West Indian expatriate fiction. Frequently, as in Lamming's work, *The Pleasures of Exile*, identity can only be found by facing this dilemma within the context of the Old World, by confrontation with the 'other'; the meeting between island and metropolis, Caliban and Prospero must occur and is a necesary prerequisite to the flowering of a real West Indian identity. Moreover, combined with the physical and psychological realities of survival in the alien city, the majority of the writers also faced the problem of overcoming the divisive effects of a colonial educational background, an education which had repeatedly told them, that 'real' places were 'cold' places and these were elsewhere:

> Everything seemed to conspire against us. The faces we saw in advertisements were not our faces; the places seen in films were not our places... the books we had to read were not our books ....Writing began and ended with Charles Dickens. He it was who determined what style ought to be and through whose eyes we saw more vividly than the tropic rain beating against our windows, the nagging London drizzle and old men warming hands over fires in musty rooms.[4]

This craving for fantasy, or a desire to create an alternative world based on the masquerade of the colonial myth had far reaching effects on the voices of this first generation of Caribbean writers who searched often in vain for the solid world of a metropolis, a world which had grown up in their imaginations on dubious and artificial literary foundations.In V.S.Naipaul's *The Mimic Men*(1968), Ralph Singh's inability to possess the heart of the city reflects the pain of the necessary process of demythologization:

> Here was the city, ...*the world*. The trams on the Embankment sparked blue....Excitement! Its heart must have lain somewhere....*I would play with famous names* as I walked the empty streets and stood on bridges. But the *magic of names* soon faded...my incantation of names remained unanswered. In the great city, so solid in its light - to me as colourless as rotten wooden fences and new corrugated iron roofs - in this solid city *life was two-dimensional*. (my italics)[5]

Similarly Sorbert, in Andrew Salkey's *Escape to an Autumn Pavement*(1960) comes to the recognition that he has not inherited a language and culture from his British colonial education but a sense of the lack of it: 'I walk around London and I see statues of this one and the other...There's even Stonehenge. And do you know how I feel deep down?...I feel nothing...We've been fed on the Mother Country myths. Its language.Its literature. Its Civics.... What happened to me between African bondage and British hypocrisy? What?'[6]

This sense of something missing, the sense of a cultural and historical void beneath the excitement that a group identity in the 'metroplis' can bring is exacerbated by the whole question of a language acquired but not possessed. As was evident from Ralph Singh's reverential incantation of names, the naming of a thing and the knowledge, understanding or possession of it can be very different things. Societies, like the individuals of which they are composed need their own areas of privacy, areas into which they can retreat and refresh themselves. For the West Indian writer abroad for whom the language as V.S.Naipaul said 'was mine' but 'the tradition was not'[7] this cycle of disillusion and cynicism is a crucial stage in the process of decolonization for it is only through this process and the reclamation of an authentic language for identity - that the writer can begin to rescue his/her community from the illusory myths of the imperial centre. And it is in this area of language -

a language for rather than against identity - that Sam Selvon's writing holds such an important and influential position.

BLACK LONDON : CITY OF WORDS

Sam Selvon's fiction set in London between the period 1950 to the mid 1980's, when he left Britain after twenty-eight years to live in Canada, is a crucial milestone in the history and development of Caribbean writing. Recently described as the 'father of Black Literature in Britain'[8] by Maya Angelou the African-American novelist, Selvon's London works - the short stories collected in *Ways of Sunlight*(1957), *The Housing Lark*(1965), a novel as its title suggests concerned with the housing problem, and the 'Moses' novels - *The Lonely Londoners*(1956), *Moses Ascending*(1975) and *Moses Migrating*(1983) - span a crucial period in the growth of black writing in Britain. With the use of a modified form of 'dialect' or what we should describe as a consciously chosen Caribbean literary English, for both the language of the narrator and that of the characters, *The Lonely Londoners* was a pioneering work as it moved towards bridging the difficult gap of perspective between the teller of the tale and the tale itself. As one of the first full-length novels to be written in this language form, it also reflected an innovative departure away from the more standard modes of portraying unlettered characters in traditional fiction. In style and content therefore it represented a major step forward in the process of decolonization.

Selvon's sojourn in London from 1950-78 acted as a creative catalyst in the development of his art enabling links to be drawn between the two preoccupations of his fiction - Trinidad and London. Through the encounter with London, it became possible to move, on the one hand, towards a more fully realised picture of the world back home and on the other, to define and establish a Caribbean consciousness within a British context. Only in 'London' says Selvon,'did my life find its purpose'.[9]

The settings of Trinidad and London have formed the major focus of Selvon's work to date. However, whilst the Indian cane community is carefully observed in the best-known Trinidad novels, *A Brighter Sun*(1952) and *Turn Again Tiger*(1957), Selvon did not come from a rural background himself nor was he 'Indianized' in any sense. Although he was born in 1923 of East Indian parents and his father was a Madrassi, Selvon related from an early age primarily to the multicultural world of modern Trinidad. Speaking of the Hindi language, he has said:

> I just ignored it...I grew up so Creolized among the Trinidadians... Not as an Indian, but as a Creolized West Indian as we say.[10]

The tensions and conflicts implicit in the idea of creolization are a frequent theme in Selvon's art whether his subject is the East Indian peasantry, the urban middle-classes, the rootless trickster figures of his London fiction or the calypsonian characters in the short stories set in Port-of-Spain. Indeed in the black London that Selvon creates in *The Lonely Londoners*(1956) we are unaware of the 'boys' particular cultural identities. So powerful is the shared dynamic of the group at this stage that even Cap, the Nigerian, begins to behave like a West Indian. Like many other immigrants of his generation, Selvon came to London to find work. Describing himself as largely self-educated he had begun his literary career as a journalist with *The Trinidad Guardian*. Soon after his arrival in London, his first novel *A Brighter Sun* was published which gained him international recognition and enabled him to become a full-time writer.

The Lonely Londoners is the first of three works dealing with the central figure of Moses Aloetta, a 'veteran' black Londoner, and his experiences with a group of ordinary and unlettered immigrants, 'black immigrants ... among whom I[Selvon] lived for a few years when I first arrived in London'.[11] As in his collection of radio plays,El Dorado West One (adaptations from *The Lonely Londoners*), the novel represents a comi-tragic attempt to subvert and demythologize the colonial dream of a bountiful city. Characteristically, Selvon's reversal of the original myth in the plays - a myth linked of course to the European voyages of discovery in the sixteenth and seventeenth centuries of the possibility of inhabiting a golden land - has several important reverberations as far as the economic base of nineteenth century imperialism and Caribbean colonial history are concerned. But Selvon's political commentary is always implicit and the world of his Londoners not gold, but grey; his questers may be led and supported by the sage figure Moses but they are limited to the bleak reality of surviving in the wilderness of an alien and alienating 'mother-country'.

At the beginning of *The Lonely Londoners*, the atmosphere of Selvon's city is described:'as if is not London at all but some strange place on another planet'.[12] Typically, the narrator subverts the standard English in the novel's opening 'One grim winter evening, when it had a kind of unrealness about London, with a fog sleeping restlessly over the city ...'(p.7) Selvon, controlling the narration and using a modified form of Caribbean English creates a distance between the narrative voice and the city whilst establishing an intimacy between the reader and the story teller. The unemployment office 'is a kind of place where hate and disgust and avarice and malice and sympathy and sorrow and pity all mix up. Is a place where everyone is your enemy and your friend'(p.22). More generally 'it have people living in London who don't know what happening in the room next to them, far more the street or how other people living...It divide up in little worlds... and you don't know anything about what happening in the other ones except what you read in the papers'(p. 74). We meet few white characters, enter few homes and topographical description is scarce yet the boundaries of Selvon's black enclave are carefully defined and always made accessible to new arrivals, who need careful initiation into the games of survival. Black London is thus domesticated by the ritualistic repetition of the names not only of important and viable areas; it is bounded for instance in the west by 'the Gate'(Notting Hill), in the east by 'the Arch'(Marble) and in the north by 'the Water'(Bayswater) but also by the stories of the 'boys' who return with exciting 'ballads' to relate after venturing out into uncharted areas of experience in the city, 'ballads' which strengthen and reinforce the fragile identity of the group's own mythology. Selvon has himself pointed out that the London these immigrants inhabited lacked any of the normal pillars of security or cohesion. His characters may see the sights or taste the bitter-sweet attractions of the metropolis but they ultimately live in a restrictive, two-dimensional world.

With its apparently unstructured episodic style and the comic dexterity of Selvon's use of a modified form of 'dialect' or what Kamau Brathwaite has more recently termed 'nation-language', the novel when it first appeared was often mistakenly regarded as being simply an amusing social documentary of West Indian manners. As such its primary intention was to reveal with pathos and compassionate irony the humorous faux pas of the black innocent abroad. The surface textures of the loosely knit sketches or 'ballads' recounted through the ambivalent voice of the third-person narrrator seemed to support this view. As readers we are swiftly drawn into the pace of the narrative and the initiation rites for the 'desperate hustlers' as they 'land up' on Moses's doorstep with 'one set of luggage, no place to sleep, no place to go'(p.8). Similarly the idiosyncracies and eccentricities of Selvon's various characters, known collectively as 'the boys' are clearly delineated. We witness the first shocks of arrival at Waterloo in the almost surrealistic opening to the novel as Moses journeys to the station through the fog of a London winter, the endless and usually abortive search for employment and the constant hunt for the forbidden fruits of 'white pussy'. The boys (the term itself suggests the almost primeval innocence of the immigrants), picaresque and calypsonian rogues from a variety of islands circle like vultures around their sage and liaison officer Moses who attempts at times to offer solace.

However from a very early stage in the novel, the romance of the city is counterpointed by a frightening sense of dislocation.

Sir Galahad's (known on arrival as Henry Oliver) initial buoyancy is fractured when he ventures out alone for the first time. The 'sun shining but Galahad never see the sun look like how it looking now. No heat from it, it just there in the sky like a force-ripe orange. When he look up, the colour of the sky so desolate it make him frighten'(p.26). Selvon's descriptions of Galahad's reactions to a different climate, particularly to the difference in the appearance of the sun, is fresh and enlightening as he uses terms of reference from a tropical world to describe the incongruities. The psychologically disorientating effects of the alien surroundings on the newcomer is created implicitly in the way the language is used. Most strikingly perhaps, the collision of the two worlds - of Trinidad and London - in Galahad's mind with the dreamlike image of the 'force-ripe orange', enables the reader to experience the extremity of Galahad's fear. Similarly by imposing the language of his subjects on the city, Selvon remakes it in their own image. At times as Gordon Rohlehr has pointed out, they shrink it by the new use of reductive analogies. The walls of Paddington slums, for example, crack like the 'last days of Pompeii'[13]

Moses's developing scepticism about the resources of this community and his urgent need to discover a private identity provide one of the major tensions in the novel as the voice of the third person narrator mediates between the consciousness of the group and the predicament of Moses himself. After a visit from Big City, who has ambitions to be a world-wide traveller, we are shown Moses's growing awareness of the futility of his existence: 'after Big City leave him Moses used to think bout... money, how it would solve all the problems in the world. He used to see all his years in London pile up one on top of the other, and he getting no place in a hurry', (p.82). Moses's sense of a pointless repetition here is significantly reflective of a voice that becomes more articulate as the novel proceeds. Set apart from the others as the sage figure, with the knowledge of years of ballads behind him, he also has to come to terms with a sense of loss. This is dramatized most clearly in his relationship with Galahad; from the opening pages at Waterloo Station Moses tries to persuade the newcomers to return 'back home' immediately. His words reveal the pain of a superior irony. Whilst Galahad's dreams of the city may be fulfilled like V.S.Naipaul's Ralph Singh in *The Mimic Men*(1967), by the phrase 'Charing Cross' or by the magnetism of Picadilly Circus, Moses's consciousness becomes increasingly disturbed. Although he attempts to relive his own past throuh Galahad's love affair with the city, he has already reached a point of stasis. As he says to Galahad,'All them places is like nothing to me now'(p.69). As Galahad's persona becomes increasingly inflated - he begins to feel more and more 'like a king living in London' - Moses is drawn further and further into his introspective reflections and desire to 'draw apart'. And the boys' protective self-caricatures and nicknames become identifiable as only a transparent form of camouflage within the black colony. Moreover, the nature of the language itself in the city of words they have created, with its reliance on repetition, drama and anecdote, can also become a regressive force - a form of restricted code with disturbing implications for the possibility of growth within or outside the community.

Selvon's 'ballad' style in *The Lonely Londoners* shifts easily between an oral and a literary tone and bears many correspondences with the native

tradition of Trinidadian calypso. The oral calypsonian ballad is well
known for its use of a subversive irony, the melodramatic exaggeration of
farcical anecdotes, racial stereotyping, repetition for dramatic effect and
the inclusion of topical political material. Also, as John Thieme has
recently shown, there are close parallels with Trinidad Carnival, a form
that is essentially 'parodic, egalitarian and subversive' but constantly
offers the possibility for renewal and regeneration. As such *The Lonely
Londoners*,he says, is a central Carnival text [14], furthermore, Carnival as a
system of discourse enables a creolization of language and form that
brings together the marketplace culture of Carnival into the world of the
printed book. Thus Selvon's attempts at literary decolonization - both
colonizes Englan' in reverse and looks forward to the later works of
Caribbean writers such as Michael Smith, Earl Lovelace, Grace Nichols,
and Linton Kwesi Johnson who combine the literary and the oral not
privileging either.

Selvon's boys then, originate in many ways from a world of
language,'a world of words through which they grope for clarity'.[15]
Sexual themes are almost always present but from a male viewpoint
(which has created critics of Selvon in recent years) though they conform
and parallel in many respects the classically chauvinistic attitudes of the
urban trickster figures of calypso. Rather like the ultimately reductive
and self-denigratory effects of their nicknames, their view of women as
'pretty pieces of skin' reflects ultimately the boys' uncertainty and
insecure sense of self.

It is partly because the conflicting values of white society reduces their
own stature that they must adopt these postures. This technique of
'naming' or 'labelling' as a means of self-defence is evident when Sir
Galahad sets off 'cool as a lord' to meet his white date and confronts the
colour problem. Never easily deflated Galahad is left talking to the
colour black as if it is a person, telling it that 'is not he who causing
botheration in the place, but Black, who is a worthless thing'(p.72).

There is no beginning or end to the experiences of 'the boys' in *The
Lonely Londoners*. Although details about Moses accumulate - we know
he is tiring of Britain and frequently dreams of a return to Trinidad - they
are unobtrusive and are fitting to his development as the novel proceeds.
The surface fragmentation or conscious disorganization of the novel's
structure therefore becomes part of its main purpose, that, 'beneath the
kiff-kiff laughter, behind the ballad and the episode, the what-
happening, the summer-is-hearts ... is a great aimlessness, a great
restless swaying movement that leaving you standing in the same
spot'(p.125). By the end of the novel Moses is aware of a meaningless
repetition and circularity in the group's existence. The phrase 'what
happening' which echoes throughout and is the fundamental rationale
of its numerous episodes, comes to imply less a resilience in the face of
complicated experience than a painful sense of futility and incoherence.

Moses's basement room which acts as a kind of surrogate religious centre is where the boys congregate every Sunday morning to swap ballads, talk about this and that but the stories are never finished and the breathless narration of this section (pp.122-5) emphasizes its lack of direction. The repartee of the community has become a self-undermining rhetoric; as the boys attempt to swap well-worn anecdotes, we witness Moses's detachment as he becomes almost a mythical repository, a Tiresias figure who can never escape the constant 'moaning and groaning and sighing and crying'. The oral and rhythmic nature of the prose adds weight to this as the synchronization of voices degenerates in to a deflationary climax which then subsides to the original theme:'So what happening these days?'Significantly the questions are not addressed to any particular subject; they ring out like voices in the wilderness.

Only Moses, who has almost merged in consciousness with the narrating voice, seems to be moving forward and can perceive the need to discover a new language for existence. The black London of Selvon's 'boys' has become by the close only a city of words: there are no firm foundations(apart from Moses's basement room), and the surface security provided by this shared code, which has reduced the vast metropolis to a manageable West Indian colony within the city will only perpetuate their isolation as there is no desire for integration. We leave Moses looking down into the River Thames and articulating this sense of a void:'when you go down a little you bounce up a misery and pathos and a kind of frightening-what? He don't have the right word but he have the right feeling in his heart'(p.126) This search for the 'right word' or an appropriate and individual voice to define a new reality for the Caribbean writer in London is central to an understanding of Selvon's first experimentations with language and form in *The Lonely Londoners* and becomes the main preoccupation of a new Moses who is still in Britain twenty years later in *Moses Ascending*(1975).

FROM BASEMENT TO ATTIC?

In *The Lonely Londoners*, Selvon faced the problem of both dealing with an early and exploratory response to the creation of a black London as well as discovering a suitable literary frame to express this experience. The slight area of narrative uncertainty in *The Lonely Londoners* is clarified in *Moses Ascending* where Moses becomes very much the self-conscious narrator. In this novel we meet a Moses who is actively trying to draw apart from all the hustling of the early days. He is now endeavouring to construct a fully-realized individual persona and at an important level - in the changed social and political climate of the 1970's, a world where the effects of oppressive Immigration Laws affect entry and departure - Moses's development is explored metaphorically. He buys his own,

admittedly delapidated house (due for demolition in three years); he is
no longer a tenant but a landlord and furthermore, he wants to be a
writer and sets out to write his Memoirs in the uppermost room with a
large view of the city, his 'castle':

> After all these years paying rent, I had the ambition to own my own property in
> London, no matter how ruinous or dilapidated it was. If you are a tenant, you
> catch your arse forever, but if you are a landlord, it is a horse of a different
> colour(p.8).

Or, as Moses says to Sir Galahad(now a fervent representative of the
Black Power movement): 'I just want to live in peace, and reap the
harvest of the years of slavery I put in Brit'n. I don't want people like you
around, to upset the applecart' (p.9)

Moses only ascends for a brief spell to live in the attic or 'penthouse' of
his own house which, as the novel proceeds, becomes increasingly
crowded with Bob (his illiterate white man Friday from the 'Black
Country') Jeannie (Bob's girlfriend and Moses's sometime mistress),
Brenda and the Black Power Group as well as some 'Pakis' who enact a
sheep slaughter in his back yard. His ambitions, to be 'Master' of his own
house and an erudite Black man of letters, suggest the possibility in
fantasy at least, of gaining security and moving away from the stasis of
the old days, the days of the 'what happening' and the 'kiff kiff
laughter'we saw in *The Lonely Londoners*. Moreover the image Moses
evokes at the opening, of gaining a 'bird's eye view' of life, is indicative of
his intention to achieve a dimension of distance on his community. But
the preservation of such a sanctuary, a literary haven in Shepherd's
Bush, is not shown to be a viable proposition, and Moses's 'castle'(p.46)
is progressivley undermined as the novel proceeds.

The atmosphere of *Moses Ascending*, like Selvon's earlier work is
initially congenial and suggests an innocently-mocking comedy
concerned with the idiosyncracies of the new generation of Third World
immigrants in the city. But Moses's attempts to separate himself from his
own community in order to make an investment in 'truth' as he calls it,
are barbed throughout by a subtly ironic method which attacks both the
aspirations of the budding black writer with his recently acquired social
graces as well as those new political radicals who make up the Black
Brit'n he now lives in. The tensions which were developing by the close
of *The Lonely Londoners* have culminated in an almost total dissipation of
the original group. The supposed security of the West Indian island in
the metropolis, the strength created by the 'boys' shared sense of
dislocation and cultural identity has collapsed. Tolroy and family are
returning to Jamaica , Big City has gone mad; he 'walks about the streets
muttering to himself, ill-kempt and unshaven...as if the whole city of
London collapse on him', others, we hear have gone up North and some

simply 'down in the underground' (p. 16) never to emerge.

Of the original group, only Galahad and Moses remain and Moses has lost much of his faith in the idea of Black unity:

> I will tell you one thing that I have learnt in this life. It is that the black man cannot unite. I have seen various causes taken up and dropped like hot coals. I have seen them come together and then scatter... in all directions(p.49).

Moses's attempts to shield himself from the suffering of his people however are not taken seriously and Galahad, as we shall see later, becomes a major contributive factor in his old friend's steady descent from his newly-won attic freedom.

Moses's developing scepticism concerning the question of commitment to an ever-continuing series of futile causes, only is comparable once again to V.S.Naipaul's *The Mimic Men*, in which Ralph Singh strives through his writing of a personal history to move beyond those sequences of false behaviour in his past which led only to a barren cycle of events. Both Selvon and Naipaul have frequently commented on the dangers for the post-colonial artist in becoming over involved in what Naipaul has termed the 'corruption of causes'[16] and Selvon too has voiced a need to develop his art further than what he regarded to be the ultimately limiting strictures and preoccupations of a literature committed in the main to the assertion of a literary nationalism. In addition his desire is to break through certain narrow interpretative categories - of 'protest','hardship'or 'slavery' - often assigned by certain metropolitan critics to the supposed naturalistic work of writers such as himself.[17] Although Selvon does not indicate a withdrawal from the black writer's struggle for acceptance in an established literary world, or that he is retreating from his responsibilities to that world 'where I belong'[18] (which now includes the whole of the Third World as well as Trinidad), he does suggest the need for an expansion of consciousness, a widening of horizons in the new literatures of the world to include grounds of more universal applicability and significance.

Interestingly,Selvon made those observations in 1979 just after his departure from Britain where he had lived for twenty-eight years, a period which also spans the creation of the Moses figure. Moses, however, does not simply present autobiography: as a representative voice of the old generation of immigrants, he typifies to Selvon 'all that happened (during that phase)... he also spoke in the idiom of the people which was the only way that he could ... express himself.' Based on a 'true-life' character, Moses, in spite of all his 'presumptions to be English... remains basically a man from the Caribbean'[19] Yet by the close of *Moses Ascending* with the growth of a new generation of Black Britons, the Black Power movement, the festering hostility between Asian immigrants and Blacks, we become aware of the impossiblity for Moses of forming an organic relationship either with his own community or the white world outside. He is outdated, a misfit, a black colonial adrift in the city, straddling or attempting to straddle both worlds.

From an early stage we are shown how Moses, with the status of a black landlord, attracts exactly those types he is attempting to avoid. Being 'unprejeudiced', his only stipulation regarding tenants is that none of the old group live in his house and he leaves all the house-management in the uncapable hands of his white Man Friday, Bob, an even-tempered, illiterate Midlands white. But the house becomes an illegal centre for the smuggling of Pakistanis into Britain and the headquarters for the local Black Power movement. Moses only becomes conscious of the real 'goings-on' in the house when he witnesses the assembly of a Black Power demonstration in the street below. Similarly his attention is first drawn to the mysterious Faizull Farouk when he hears the bleating of a sheep - a victim for a Muslim sacrifice - in his backyard.

Whilst Moses's lack of awareness is treated humorously, his predicament has several disturbing implications. The episode of the sheep-slaughter for instance is representative of the seriousness of Moses's new situation. On one level, the description of this scene is a successfully comical account of an absurd event which is symtomatic of the confused clash of cultural values affecting the new generation of immigrants in Britain. Moses is interested in the episode only because Galahad has pressurized him to research topical material for his writing. The 'Pakis' are religiose about the whole affair and attempt to adhere strictly to Muslim rituals. In contrast, Bob, watching from a window upstairs reacts with horror:

> A solitary shriek of horror rent the atmosphere. It was so unexpected and piercing that Faizull lose his grip and slip off the sheep...I was the onlyest one to keep my cool: I look up to the penthouse and see Bob leaning out of the window as if he vomiting. 'I will get the RSPCA to arrest you!' He shout, 'You too, Moses!' Everything was going nice and smooth until this white man run amok.(p.63).

The position of Moses in relation to Bob compares interestingly here with that of Moses and Galahad in *The Lonely Londoners* when Galahad tells Moses the 'ballad' of his attempt to catch a pigeon for his supper in Kensington Gardens. There is obviously one major cultural difference between the two episodes and that is Bob's conventional English attitude concerning cruelty to animals and Galahad's perspective as a human being who is starving in a strange world where animals(even pigeons) grow fat whilst human beings starve. Bob's lack of familiarity with the cultural context of what he sees curiously parallels that of Galahad when confronted with a universe of cossetted dogs and protected pigeons; a world with different emphases of value. But, most importantly, this parallel involves a further contrast: that between Moses as confidant or fellow West Indian in *The Lonely Londoners* and Moses as landlord having to accommodate the sensibilities of a native Englishman in *Moses Ascending*. From being simply an outsider listening to those similar to himself, Moses has moved in to the more complicated position of attempting to be an insider with responsibilities both to his tenants and his neighbours which require him to mediate between the black and white worlds. He therefore cannot remain the easy-going black radical of the early days; he is now a man with vested interests who desires to fit in and to find a place in British society. This desire is emphasized by the exaggerated adoption of certain British customs which he considers to be proper to his class, such as a drinks cupboard and a white manservant. This difference is further exaggerated by the language he speaks.

Moses's literary ambitiousness is gently parodied by Selvon, his faith in his ability to write 'Queen's English' is shown to be not that dissimilar to his recent rise in social status and the language he uses further reflects the hybrid nature of his personality. The first person narration modulates between the formality of nineteenth century English, Trinidadian proverbs, Greek myth, American films, contemporary advertising jingles to the banter of the old days. Selvon's linguistic resourcefulness, his subversion of the 'Standard' and his iconoclastic methods which unite both calypso with Western literature, only serve to heighten our awareness that Moses can not yet fully inhabit a 'home'; he is not yet Master of his own house or of the language with which he wants to compose his Memoirs. Furthermore his partial misunderstanding of many of the terms he is trying to appropriate reflects once again the divisive effects of the acquisition of a second-hand language a language used but not possessed. Moses, is not trying to own the 'magical' heart of the city but he is attempting to become a writer and in doing so needs to discover an appropriate voice.

Selvon's portrayal of Moses's attempts to find a voice is one of total confusion: a confusion of notions of order and reality, and the creation of a conglomeration which one reviewer called a 'verbal salad of ungrammatical wit and literary and biblical references'[20]. However, whilst the iconoclastic effects of this hybrid language may be inspired, as in the following extract describing again the sheep slaughter,

> Kay sir rah, sir rah, as the Japanese say. It was a motley trio Faizull shepherd into the house. I have seen bewildered adventurers land in Waterloo from the Caribbean with all their incongrous paraphernalia and myriad expressions of amazement and shock, but this Asian threesome beat them hands down (p. 74).

the result is ultimately one of pathos. Similarly in Moses's innovative, highly ironic and lyrical 'essay' which he composes to the Black man early in the novel (pp.11-15) the only coherent piece he manages to complete before Galahad's Black Power pressure disturbs him, we see the means by which Moses's potentially serious and political subject-matter is parodied by Selvon and rendered absurd by his literary style.

The essay deals with the plight of black workers in a hostile white urban society (quoted from earlier in the first section of this essay), a position of deprivation and inequality, and an issue that might have most naturally found expression in a polemical attack. Yet Selvon's technique and the quality of the pathos that results moves beyond the basic facts of the issue itself. In its wide range of 'literary' effects and the eccentric usage of a mixture of 'literary' terms, the piece which is too long to quote fully here, mirrors the growth of Moses's linguistic affectations since his retirement. Moses's range incorporates nation language, standard English, the Shakespearian 'Fie' or 'Gods blood things have come to a pretty pass', as well as references by allusion to historic moments such as the 'Black Watch'. At times, Moses even uses a modified form of Caribbean English to describe the white man's predicament. This conglomeration of linguistic modes and Moses's very sincere attempt to write in the argumentative style of the traditional essay form, an attempt which achieves precisely the opposite effect is typical of the novel as a whole. Whilst Moses sets out to present us with all the advantages of the black worker's position, he establishes with innocent elegance a very different picture.

Moses Ascending is very much a novelist's novel. There are explicit references by Moses, the fictional author, to other real Caribbean writers living in London - George Lamming and Andrew Salkey for instance - but more significantly, the predominant tension in the book stems from Moses's attempts to actually become a black writer and to establish an authentic voice that his own people will listen to. The novel therefore dramatises the difficulties Moses faces as a black post-colonial writer in Britain. After careful study of the pros and cons of the writing process, Moses begins to feel that he ought to be able to write a book with a proper plot and theme. Furthermore he must reveal the breadth of his education and knowledge by using a language that can incorporate for instance classical myth, legend, the bible and oral folklore. The result is, as Michel Fabre has pointed out,'the sophisticated appropriation by 'colonial writing' of a literary style formerly reserved for the British born.' Moses's voice reflects almost a carnivalization of language as he blends outdated, jerky phrases with Trinidadian syntactical shifts and turns. Through Moses as a 'writer-of-memoirs', Selvon as a novelist claims the right to depart from the naturalistic ways of using English usually prescribed to non-British writers....[he] does not assimilate into the ...mainstream, he explodes it'.[21]

Moses's relationship with Sir Galahad and the Black Power movement is also instructive. Throughout the novel, the development of Moses's private identity is threatened by the public and political world of Brenda and Galahad and the avidly supported Black Power group. Moses does not withdraw completely from them (it is he in fact who acts when the 'Party' does not have enough money to rescue two of its innocent brethren jailed after an unfortunate encounter with the police). Yet, paradoxically, Moses's remaining sense of incompleteness and a doubting of his selfhood is created most strongly by the pressures his own people impose on him. It is because he is a black writer that the conflict between his personal wishes to write his Memoirs and the demands made upon him by a fast-developing political situation are exaggerated. As Moses becomes increasingly plagued by what his 'proper' subject should be, his private work is gradually stultified, and he through conscience becomes involved in events which do not really concern him. Furthermore the possibility of further withdrawal is no longer a viable alternative.

Galahad and Brenda will not accept Moses's refusal to be involved in what he calls the 'bandwagon' of Black Power. Moses regards the new movement only as an alternative to more 'ballads' and 'episodes', 'liming' or roaming the streets. Galahad, the political activist is ridiculed by the narrator's wider vision which penetrates beneath his Black Power 'glad rags' and the use of the latest political jargon to expose a still profoundly vulnerable awareness of self. Selvon gently exposes the corruption at the centre of the party but it is in Galahad's harsh criticisms of Moses's writing that Selvon pinpoints the serious damage which Galahad's unconscious self-contempt reveals. Furthermore it undermines Moses himself who begins to feel like a traitor:

> 'What shit is that you writing?' [Galahad]
> 'I am composing my Memoirs', I say stiffly...
> 'You don't know one fucking thing about what's happening, Moses'.
> 'Memoirs are personal and intimate...
> 'That's no ... use...nobody ain't going to be interested in anything you have to say. If you was writing about the scene today,and the struggle, I might of got the Party to back you. In any case, who tell you you could write?'
> 'I am not an ignoramus like you', I say beginning to lose my cool.
> 'You think writing book is like kissing hand? You should leave that to people like Lamming and Salkey.'
> 'Who?'
> 'You see what I mean? Man, Moses you are still living in the Dark Ages. You don't even know we have created a Black Literature...'(pp.49-50).

This confrontation between Galahad and Moses is perhaps the most explicit demonstration in the novel of Selvon's concern to explore the difficulties facing the writer who remains abroad.

Moses Ascending does not present the reader with any comfortable resolutions but a sense of continuity is created by Selvon's demonstration of the impossibility for the post-colonial writer in Moses's circumstances to achieve such an end. Selvon repeatedly emphasizes the absurdity of the whole situation and Moses's movements in the novel (whether upwards or sideways) create a cyclical ironic pattern framed by the 'goings-on' in the house and culminating in Moses's final return to life in his own basement room. At one level Moses seems only to have moved from basement to attic and back again during his twenty-odd years in Britain; he is still living an underground existence and his fall from power at the close of the novel almost verges on the tragic. But Selvon's ambiguous ironic tone holds good even in this final moment of humiliation when Bob, Brenda and 'Paki' have all turned against him to further their own interests:

> Thus are the mighty fallen, empires totter, monarchs dethrone and the walls of Pompeii bite the dust. Humiliated and degraded I took up abode in Bob's erstwhile room while he and Jeannie moved in to the Penthouse.(p.143)

Having failed to set up home in a city of words, Moses resolves to sell up and return to Trinidad. The gauntlet that he flings at his former tenants in the form of an 'epilogue up his sleeve' becomes the central theme of *Moses Migrating* in which Moses finally decides to leave London and return home for Carnival. The novel opens with the reality of departure and is illustrative of Selvon's continuing preoccupation with the theme of the exile's displacement and the lack of a firm centre as Moses writes a concerned letter to Enoch Powell thanking him for his generosity in helping Black Londoners to return to their native lands:

> Dear Mr Powell, though Black I am writing you to express my support for your campaigns to keep Brit'n White... I have always tried to integrate successfully in spite of discriminations and prejudices according to race etc...(p.1)[22]

The comic-grotesque reversals of the colonial encounter are developed as Moses, travelling third class in a liner - Selvon mock-seriously invokes the trials of the Middle Passage - ends up in the literally 'upside-down' world of the Trinidad Hilton - a tourist, in other words in his own country. The metaphorical possibilities of rooms and houses as a correlative or frame for the lack of a firm cultural identity are thus extended; but it is neither basement nor attic but hotel room which bears the weight of significance. The quintessential transitoriness, artificiality and unreality of the hotel room (under ground too) image the special hollowness and disorientations of Moses's post-colonial identity. Moses seems fated to find no true home in either Britain or Trinidad. No more than in *The Lonely Londoners* or *Moses Ascending* does Selvon's character arrive at a promised land. The lack of a resolution, and perhaps the lack of a possible resolution, is demonstrated in the open-ended quality of the novel's final episode - with Moses caught at the close in a kind of suspended state, just outside the doors of Heathrow airport 'like I was still playing charades' (p.179).

NOTES

1. Sam Selvon, *Moses Ascending* (London: Davis Poynter, 1975), pp.6-7. All further references are to this edition and are included in the text.
2. Jean Rhys,*Voyage in the Dark* (Harmondsworth : Penguin,1975),p.7
3. Donald Hinds,*Journey to an Illusion* (London:1966) ,p.4
4. Shiva Naipaul, 'The Writer Without a Society', in *Common Wealth*, edited by Anna Rutherford (Aarhus : Akademisk Boghandel, 1971), pp.115-16.
5. V.S.Naipaul, *The Mimic Men* (Harmondsworth : Penguin, ,1972), pp. 18-19.
6. Andrew Salkey, *Escape to An Autumn Pavement* (London : Hutchinson, 1960) , p.46.
7. V.S.Naipaul,' Jasmine', in *The Overcrowded Baracoon* (Harmonsworth : Penguin paperback edtn.,1976), p.27.
8. Maya Angelou, in conversation with Susheila Nasta: unpublished.
9. Michel Fabre, 'Samuel Selvon: Interviews and Conversations', in *Critical Perspectives on Sam Selvon*, ed. Susheila Nasta (Washington, 1988), p.64.
10. Gerald Moore, 'The English Novel Abroad', (BBC Broadcast, Jan 4,1974).
11. Peter Nazareth, 'Interview with Sam Selvon', in *World Literature in English*, Vol 18, No.2 (1979), p.421.
12. Sam Selvon, *The Lonely Londoners* (London : Longman,1956). All further references are to this edition and are included in the text.
13. Gordon Rohlehr, 'The Folk in Caribbean Literature' (*Tapia*,Dec 17,1972), p.14.
14. John Thieme, 'The World Turn Upside Down:Carnival Patterns in *The Lonely Londoners*' (*Toronto South-Asian Review*,5,1,1986),p.194.
15. Gordon Rohlehr, p.15
16. V.S.Naipaul, *The Overcrowded Baracoon*. (Harmondsworth : Penguin paperback edtn.,1976).
17. Peter Nazareth, 'Interview with Sam Selvon', in *World Literature Written in English*, 18, 2 (1979), p.430-1.
18. *Ibid.*
19. Frank Birbalsingh, 'Interview with Sam Selvon' (unpublished; thanks to the author).
20. Jill Neville,*The Sunday Times*,Aug.24,1975,p.25.
21. Michel Fabre,'Sam Selvon', in *West Indian Literature*, ed. Bruce King,(London : Macmillan, 1979), p.123.
22. Samuel Selvon, *Moses Migrating* (London : Longman, 1983), p.1.

SAM SELVON

My Girl and the City (1957)

All these words that I hope to write, I have written them already many times in my mind. I have had many beginnings, each as good or as bad as the other. Hurtling in the underground from station to station, mind the doors, missed it!, there is no substitute for wool: waiting for a bus in Piccadilly Circus: walking across the Waterloo Bridge: watching the bed of the Thames when the tide is out - choose one, choose a time, a place, any time or any place, and take off, as if this were interrupted conversation, as if you and I were earnest friends and there is no need for preliminary remark.

One day of any day it is like this. I wait for my girl on Waterloo Bridge, and when she comes there is a mighty wind blowing across the river, and we lean against it and laugh, her skirt skylarking, her hair whipping across her face.

I wooed my girl, mostly on her way home from work, and I talked a great deal. Often, it was as if I had never spoken, I heard my words echo in deep caverns of thought, as if they hung about like cigarette smoke in a still room, missionless; or else they were lost for ever in the sounds of the city.

We used to wait for a 196 under the railway bridge across the Waterloo road. There were always long queues and it looked like we would never get a bus. Fidgeting in that line of impatient humanity I got in precious words edgeways, and a train would rumble and drown my words in thundering steel. Still, it was important to talk. In the crowded bus, as if I wooed three or four instead of one, I shot words over my shoulder, across seats; once past a bespectacled man reading the *Evening News* who lowered his paper and eyed me that I was mad. My words bumped against people's faces, on the glass window of the bus; they found passage between 'fares please' and once I got to writing things on a piece of paper and pushing my hand over two seats.

The journey ended, there was urgent need to communicate before we parted.

All these things I say, I said, waving my hand in the air as if to catch the words floating about me and give them mission. I say them because I want you to know, I don't ever want to regret afterwards that I didn't say enough, I would rather say too much.

Take that Saturday evening, I am waiting for her in Victoria station. When she comes we take the Northern Line to Belsize Park (I know a way to the heath from there, I said). When we get out of the lift and step outside there is a sudden downpour and everyone scampers back into the station. We wait a while, then go out in it. We get lost. I say, Let us ask that fellow the way. But she says No, fancy asking someone the way to the heath on this rainy night, just find out how to get back to the tube station.

We go back, I get my bearings afresh, and we set off. She is hungry. Wait here, I say under a tree at the side of the road, and I go to a pub for some sandwiches. Water slips off me and makes puddles on the counter as I place my order. The man is taking a long time and I go to the door and wave to her across the street signifying I shan't be too long.

When I go out she has crossed the road and is sheltering in a doorway pouting. You leave me standing in the rain and stay such a long time, she says. I had to wait for the sandwiches, I say, what do you think, I was having a quick one? Yes, she says.

We walk on through the rain and we get to the heath and the rain is falling slantways and carefree and miserable. For a minute we move around in an indecisive way as if we're looking for some particular spot. Then we see a tree which might offer some shelter and we go there and sit on a bench wet and bedraggled.

I am sorry for all this rain, I say, as if I were responsible. I take off her raincoat and make her put on my quilted jacket. She takes off her soaking shoes and tucks her feet under her skirt on the bench. She tries to dry her hair with a handkerchief. I offer her the sandwiches and light a cigarette for myself. Go on, have one, she says. I take a half and munch it, and smoke.

It is cold there. The wind is raging in the leaves of the trees, and the rain is pelting. But abruptly it ceases, the clouds break up in the sky, and the moon shines. When the moon shines, it shines on her face, and I look at her, the beauty of her washed by rain, and I think many things.

Suddenly we are kissing and I wish I could die there and then and there's an end to everything, to all the Jesus-Christ thoughts that make up every moment of my existence.

Writing all this now - and some weeks have gone by since I started - it is lifeless and insipid and useless. Only at the time, there was something, a thought that propelled me. Always, in looking back, there was something, and at the time I am aware of it, and the creation goes on and on in my mind while I look at all the faces around me in the tube, the restless rustle of newspapers, the hiss of air as the doors close, the enaction of life in a variety of form.

Once I told her and she said, as she was a stenographer, that she would come with me and we would ride the Inner Circle and I would just voice my thoughts and she would write them down, and that way we could make something of it. Once the train was crowded and she sat opposite to me and after a while I looked at her and she smiled and turned away. What is all this, what is the meaning of all these things that happen to people, the movement from one place to another, lighting a cigarette, slipping a coin into a slot and pulling a drawer for chocolate, buying a return ticket, waiting for a bus, working the crossword puzzle in the *Evening Standard?*

Sometimes you are in the underground and you have no idea what the weather is like, and the train shoots out of a tunnel and sunlight floods you, falls across your newspaper, makes the passengers squint and look up.

There is a face you have for sitting at home and talking, there is a face you have for working in the office, there is a face, a bearing, a demeanour for each time and place. There is above all a face for travelling, and when you have seen one you have seen all. In a rush hour, when we are breathing down each other's neck, we look at each other and glance quickly away. There is not a great deal to look at in the narrow confines of a carriage except people, and the faces of people, but no one deserves a glass of Hall's wine more than you do. We jostle in the subway from train to lift; we wait, shifting our feet. When we are all herded inside we hear the footsteps of a straggler for whom the operator waits, and we try to figure out what sort of a footstep it is, if he feels the lift will wait for him; we are glad if he is left waiting while we shoot upward. Out of the lift, down the street, up the road: in ten seconds flat it is over, and we have to begin again.

One morning I am coming into the city by the night bus 287 from Streatham. It is after one o'clock; I have been stranded again after seeing my girl home. When we get to Westminster bridge the sky is marvellously clear with a few stray patches of beautiful cloud among which stars sparkle. The moon stands over Waterloo bridge, above the Houses of Parliament sharply outlined, and it throws gold on the waters of the Thames. The Embankment is quiet, only a few people loiter around the public convenience near to the Charing Cross underground which is open all night. A man sleeps on a bench. His head is resting under headlines: Suez Deadlock.

Going back to that same spot about five o'clock in the evening, there was absolutely nothing to recall the atmosphere of the early morning hours. Life had taken over completely, and there was nothing but people. People waiting for buses, people hustling for trains.

I go to Waterloo bridge and they come pouring out of the offices and they bob up and down as they walk across the bridge. From the station green trains come and go relentlessly. Motion mesmerizes me into immobility. There are lines of motion across the river, on the river.

Sometimes we sat on a bench near the river, and if the tide was out you could see the muddy bed of the river and the swans grubbing. Such spots, when found, are pleasant to loiter in. Sitting in one of those places - choose one, and choose a time - where it is possible to escape for a brief spell from Christ and the cup of tea. I have known a great frustration and weariness. All these things, said, have been said before, the river seen, the skirt pressed against the swelling thigh noted, the lunch hour eating apples in the sphinx's lap under Cleopatra's Needle observed and duly registered: even to talk of the frustration is a repetition. What am I to do, am I to take each circumstance, each thing seen, noted, and mill them in my mind and spit out something entirely different from the reality?

My girl is very real. She hated the city, I don't know why. It's like that sometimes, a person doesn't have to have a reason. A lot of people don't like London that way, you ask them why and they shrug, and a shrug is sometimes a powerful reply to a question.

She shrugged when I asked her why, and when she asked me why I loved London I too shrugged. But after a minute I thought I would try to explain, because too often a shrug is an easy way out of a lot of things.

Falteringly I told her how one night it was late and I found a fish and chips shop open in the East End and I bought and ate in the dark street walking; and of the cup of tea in an all-night café in Kensington one grim winter morning; and of the first time I ever queued in this country in '50 to see the Swan Lake ballet, and the friend who was with me gave a busker two and six because he was playing Sentimental Journey on a mouth-organ.

But why do you love London, she said.

You can't talk about a thing like that, not really. Maybe I could have told her because one evening in the summer I was waiting for her, only it wasn't like summer at all. Rain had been falling all day, and a haze hung about the bridges across the river, and the water was muddy and brown, and there was a kind of wistfulness and sadness about the evening. The way St Paul's was, half-hidden in the rain, the motionless trees along the Embankment. But you say a thing like that and people don't understand at all. How sometimes a surge of greatness could sweep over you when you see something.

But even if I had said all that and much more, it would not have been what I meant. You could be lonely as hell in the city, then one day you look around you and you realise everybody else is lonely too, withdrawn, locked, rushing home out of the chaos: blank faces, unseeing eyes, millions and millions of them, up the Strand, down the Strand, jostling in Charing Cross for the 5.20: in Victoria station, a pretty continental girl wearing a light, becoming shade of lipstick stands away from the board on which the departure of trains appear and cocks her head sideways, hands thrust into pockets of a fawn raincoat.

I catch the eyes of this girl with my own: we each register sight, appreciation: we look away, our eyes pick up casual station activities: she turns to an automatic refreshment machine, hesitant, not sure if she would be able to operate it.

Things happen, and are finished with for ever: I did not talk to her, I did not look her way again, or even think of her.

I look on the wall of the station at the clock, it is after half-past eight, and my girl was to have met me since six o'clock. I feel in my pockets for pennies to telephone. I only have two. I ask change of a stander with the usual embarrassment: when I telephone, the line is engaged. I alternate between standing in the spot we have arranged to meet and telephoning, but each time the line is engaged. I call the exchange: they ascertain that something is wrong with the line.

At ten minutes to nine I am eating a cornedbeef sandwich when she comes. Suddenly now nothing matters except that she is here. She never expected that I would still be waiting, but she came on the offchance. I never expected that she would come, but I waited on the offchance.

Now I have a different word for this thing that happened - an offchance, but that does not explain why it happens, and what it is that really happens. We go to St James's Park, we sit under a tree, we kiss, the moon can be seen between leaves.

Wooing my way towards, sometimes in our casual conversation we came near to great, fundamental truths, and it was a little frightening. It wasn't like wooing at all, it was more discussion of when will it end, and must it ever end, and how did it begin, and how go on from here? We scattered words on the green summer grass, under trees, on dry leaves in a wood of quivering aspens, and sometimes it was as if I was struck speechless with too much to say, and held my tongue between thoughts frightened of utterance.

Once again I am on a green train returning to the heart from the suburbs, and I look out of window into windows of private lives flashed on my brain. Bread being sliced, a man taking off a jacket, an old woman knitting. And all these things I see - the curve of a woman's arm, undressing, the blankets being tucked, and once a solitary figure staring at trains as I stared at windows. All the way into London Bridge—is falling down, is falling down, the wheels say: one must have a thought - where buildings and the shadows of them encroach on the railway tracks. Now the train crawls across the bridges, dark steel in the darkness: the thoughtful gloom of Waterloo: Charing Cross bridge, Thames reflecting lights, and the silhouettes of city buildings against the sky of the night.

When I was in New York, many times I went into that city late at night after a sally to the outskirts, it lighted up with a million lights, but never a feeling as on entering London. Each return to the city is loaded with thought, so that by the time I take the Inner Circle I am as light as air.

At last I think I know what it is all about. I move around in a world of words. Everything that happens is words. But pure expression is nothing. One must build on the things that happen: it is insufficient to say I sat in the underground and the train hurtled through the darkness and someone isn't using Amplex. So what? So now I weave, I say there was an old man on whose face wrinkles rivered, whose hands were shapeful with arthritis but when he spoke, oddly enough, his voice was young and gay.

But there was no old man, there was nothing, and there is never ever anything.

My girl, she is beautiful to look at. I have seen her in sunlight and in moonlight, and her face carves an exquisite shape in darkness.

These things we talk, I burst out, why musn't I say them?

If I love you, why shouldn't I tell you so?

I love London, she said.

ROYDON SALICK

Selvon and the Limits of Heroism:
A Reading of *The Plains of Caroni*

In an attempt, to use the author's own words, 'to project my part of the world onto the map because I found when I went to live in England that people never knew where Trinidad was', Samuel Selvon has created a literature of short stories and novels that portray the lives of essentially three kinds of character - country-bound peasants, middle-class Trinidadians living in Trinidad, and lower-class West Indian immigrants, lured to London by the grandiose expectations of an inverted El Dorado myth. Criticism has, to a large extent, neglected the middle - class Trinidadian who appears in *An Island Is a World* (1955) and *I Hear Thunder* (1963), the former considered by the author to be his most ambitious, and in some ways his most important work. These two novels have as their protagonists mainly creolized Indo-Trinidadians, who in an attempt to find themselves, experience 'the existential and metaphysical crisis of an educated and professional group of middle-class Trinidadians in post-war years'[1] .The bulk of criticism has focused on the peasant novels and the immigrant novels. The peasant novels are about the Indo-Trinidadian peasant in his local milieu, and the immigrant novels, except for one, are all set in London and its environs, and are generally about the Afro-West Indian, and specifically about the Afro-Trinidadian.

    The lush rural landscapes of the peasant novels are decidedly different from the sombre, hazy backdrop of London. The warmth and colour of the former give way to the cool, grey shades of the immigrant novels. Moreover, a sense that life consists of a constant struggling for and away from land and cane pervades the peasant novels, while humour, sexual indulgence and hustling characterize the immigrant works. A consistently overlooked aspect of the peasant novels is the noticeable absence of the quality of humour that is, in a real sense, at the heart of the immigrant novels. The difference, I believe, is a sure indication of the cultural disparity between the two largest ethnic groups that are, in one way or another, the primary focus of much of Selvon's writing. No other writer devotes so much of his fiction to the implications and modalities of the relations between Indo-Trinidadians and Afro-Trinidadians.

In the immigrant novels - *The Housing Lark* (1965), *The Lonely Londoners* (1956), *Moses Ascending* (1975), and *Moses Migrating* (1983) - there is an obvious, perhaps intentional irony that substantially undercuts the possibilities of real achievement in the lives of the protagonists. *The Housing Lark* is not easy to assess, simply because it is difficult to know exactly what Selvon was trying to do in it. There appears to be some attempt to vindicate the primacy of the human imagination, but the novel remains too much of a *jeu d'esprit* to comfortably accommodate a reading centred around achievement or heroism, in spite of the fact that the house is finally secured on the strength of the painstaking saving of the group of six West Indian immigrants, and more significantly, on the projected earnings of calypsonian Harry Banjo. It is worth noting that Selvon accords the women, especially Teena, a pivotal and decisive role in the novel.

There is, as well, something obviously anti-heroic about the immigrant novels, especially when considered contextually. Thus at the end of *The Lonely Londoners,* Moses after all the fêtes, the constant counselling and the sexual indulgence, is at his loneliest, threatening to be overwhelmed by a massive meaninglessness:

> Under the kiff-kiff laughter, behind the ballad and the episode, the what-happening, the summer-is hearts, he could see a great aimlessness, a great restless, swaying movement that leaving you standing in the same spot. As if a forlorn shadow of doom fall on all the spades in the country. As if he could see the black faces bobbing up and down in the millions of white, strained faces, everybody hustling along the Strand, the spades jostling in the crowd, bewildered hopeless. (p.141).

Kenneth Ramchand is right when he alerts us to 'Moses' individuation and his emergence as a thinking creature',[2] but this does not gainsay the awful loneliness of the narrator's final comment: 'it was the sort of night that if you wasn't making love to a woman you *feel* you was the only person in the world like that' [my italics]. Indeed the sentence only increases the frightening loneliness; and there is a deliberate moving away from 'cogitations' to feeling.

When Moses reappears, some twenty years later, in *Moses Ascending,* the reader is struck not by the similarity but by the difference between the new Moses and the Moses of *The Lonely Londoners.* Although Selvon takes great pains to convince us that it is the same character, we are not easily convinced. Our difficulty springs from Selvon's attempt to work backwards; for in a real sense the Moses of *The Lonely Londoners* appears an older, wiser, chastened and reflective character. Indeed, he is the composite of all three protagonists. If I may be permitted a musical metaphor: *Moses Ascending* is the *scherzo, Moses Migrating,* the *brio,* and *The Lonely Londoners,* the *adagio piu grave* of Selvon's metropolitan opus.

Moses Ascending plots the simultaneous rise and fall of the protagonist:

we watch as Moses becomes materially comfortable, while at the same time we sense his moral and spiritual decline. Moses can hardly be Ramchand's 'thinking creature' in this work, because he cannot grasp his moral decline. The final and centripetal irony shows Moses descending into a basement apartment, becoming in the process an improbable mixture of landlord and tenant. The view from his basement window suggests the bleakness of his future prospects, and the imagery invites our scrutiny: 'I surveyed the miniature jungle I could see out of the window, wondering if I should start all over again, forage among the undergrowth and grub for acorns and truffles' (p.138). Selvon's chastisement of his protagonist is markedly clear: Moses has permitted a diminution and corruption of his humanity. Although the fictional contexts are, *prima facie*, quite different, Moses' journey is somewhat like that of Kurtz, regressive and atavastic.

Moses Migrating, the most critical of the trilogy, reveals the inability of Moses to return to meaningful living in his homeland in spite of the love of a good woman and the support of a caring aunt who raised him. Although Carnival is open enough to encourage and allow any mimetic experiments, Moses' obsessive desire to masquerade as Britannia is not without its trenchant irony. The final image of Moses, standing at the London immigration counter holding 'the silver cup he won as first prize for his impersonation of Britain', is made more resonant by the comparison with the Holy Grail. The deliberate comparison serves to suggest the chasm separating true epic heroism and Moses' mere mimicry of such conduct. It also suggests the distance between the significance of glorious achievement attendant upon arduous struggle and the commercial rewards of masquerading.

The Moses trilogy then shows quite patently the rootlessness of many characters, especially of the protagonist, Moses Aloetta, who is unable, because of a profound confusion of values, to find either peace of mind or spiritual or emotional fulfilment anywhere. London continually rejects him; although he finds love and warmth there, he rejects, somewhat wilfully, his homeland. Morally bankrupt and culturally marooned, Moses must forever face the 'great aimlessness'.

In the peasant novels, however, *A Brighter Sun* (1952), its sequel, *Turn Again Tiger* (1958), and *The Plains of Caroni* (1970), Selvon treats of the theme of the possibilities of heroism, for in these three novels, especially in the first and the last, we sense the apotheosis of the Indo-Trinidadian peasant. I have argued elsewhere that Tiger Baboolal may be seen as a latter-day, Caribbeanized version of the epic heroes of old. For Tiger has, along with an obsessive desire to know as much as he can, an epic longing to found a racially integrated and politically independent Trinidad. Although there is the occasional admonishment of the hero, there is also the general approbation of Tiger's painful journey out of insularity and illiteracy into the harsh but rewarding light of manhood and knowledge. Fortunately, his academic pursuit, still inchoate but categorically not banal, do not take him away from the land, the source of pride, of livelihood and of anguish for his kind. As Tiger faces a future limitless in promise, he is a chastened young man with the sure knowledge of the planting cycle and significantly with the secret mystery of words. Tiger's confident odyssey is unobtrusively but perfectly adumbrated in the final affirmation of the novel, 'Now is a good time to plant corn'. The careful reader remembers that Tiger's first words to Sookdeo, to Urmilla, to Ramlal, to Boysie and to the men in the rumshop were all questions. The calculated shift from initial question to final assertion is an index of Tiger's growth in self-assurance and knowledge.

In *Turn Again Tiger*, written six years after *A Brighter Sun*, Selvon, after a novel about the middle-class professional Trinidadian, and another about immigrant life in London, returns to the peasant as hero. *Turn Again Tiger* is quite a surprising novel, since it is meant to be a sequel to *A Brighter Sun*. Indeed, Selvon, who admits to working quickly, appears to have trouble with sequels. Naipaul may very well be right in his assessment that Selvon does not have the stamina for a full-length novel. [3] Selvon is at his best in short stories and vignettes; and this accounts for the brilliance of individual portions of novels and for a lurking dissatisfaction with the whole. In *Turn Again Tiger*, Tiger against his vow to his wife, made at the end of *A Brighter Sun*, returns to the cane-fields, not in Chaguanas but in Five Rivers, as a bookkeeper/ foreman of an experimental cane plantation. Against his better judgement and against all that his bitter struggle in *A Brighter Sun* signifies, Tiger agrees to help his father manage a cane plantation. It may be that Selvon's point is that the Indo-Trinidadian peasant, represented by Tiger, who, we recall, comes from Chaguanas, *the* Indian area of Trinidad, cannot *votively* eradicate the cane experience from his life. He must first come to terms with what sugar cane, the most ubiquitous existential symbol of Caribbean race relations, really means. He must first come to terms with the inherent ambivalence of cane, the means of livelihood and honest toil for generations of Indians, but also the great impediment to their progress in a plural society, an ambivalence so well illustrated in the short story. *Cane Is Bitter* and in *The Plains of Caroni*. The pivotal incident in *Turn Again Tiger* is quite a surprising one - the sexual encounter between Tiger and Doreen Robinson, wife of the white plantation overseer. Nothing in the development of Tiger prepares us for this. To be inflamed by stumbling on a white woman bathing naked in a stream is one thing, but to pursue and virtually rape her is another altogether. Selvon sacrifices realism here for symbolism, albeit a heavy-handed symbolism, and thus relinquishes his strength as a writer: the ability to create characters and situations rich in idiosyncratic life.

Nothing comes from this encounter - neither pleasure, nor peace of mind, nor satisfaction. In fact, Tiger is far more troubled than he ever was; his inner turmoil resulting from this gratuitous act is so great that it compels him to perform another surprising act, that of burning all his books. We are meant to accept that such a hard-earned and jealously-guarded prize as knowledge, symbolized by books, can be so easily destroyed. Tiger also begins to drink heavily, and this coupled with his admixture of guilt, revenge and anger over his encounter with Doreen, leads him away from everything he holds dear. Tiger sees his promise to his father through, and so the experimental case is harvested, though not without unforeseen problems. We leave *Turn Again Tiger* feeling that Tiger's integrity has been compromised.

It is a curious fact that while Tiger plunges into despair and futile doubt, Urmilla, his wife, comes gradually into her own. Surprisingly, Tiger, maturing more slowly, senses Urmilla's need for self-assertion, and he is moved by her leading the village women to force a reduction in the consumption of alcohol and to demand more attention from their husbands. Where the other women fail, she succeeds. At the end of the novel, she is rich with her second child, having established some measure of self-assurance and confidence. Though we may not see her as an earth goddess, as one adventurous critic does, [4] we sense that she has matured sufficiently to know what independent life entails.

The Tiger saga, in an important way, continues in *The Plains of Caroni*, a book that resulted from an eighteen-month stay in Trinidad, when Selvon was paid by Tate & Lyle, the British sugar conglomerate, to write a book about the sugar industry in Trinidad. Although Selvon spent his longest return visit in Tacarigua, where incidentally *Turn Again Tiger* is set, he chose to set his new novel in Wilderness, more than likely a fictionalized version of Warrenville, a village six miles north east of Chaguanas. It was here that an incident over the introduction of the mechanical harvester occurred in 1968, an incident in which shots were fired without injury. This is the historical quarry from which Selvon partially drew his material for his most heroic, and sadly, his most neglected novel, since to date, only a few short reviews have appeared. *The Plains of Caroni* was republished in 1985 to introduce a recently-migrated Selvon to the Canadian public. Evidently, the event went unnoticed, for the Canadian literary world was silent. This, therefore, is the first sustained analysis accorded *The Plains of Caroni*, which one reviewer calls Selvon's 'finest book'. [5]

The heroic impulse which impels *A Brighter Sun* resurfaces in *The Plains of Caroni*, but in the later novel it is channelled through two different characters, one young, the other old. Selvon creates two heroes, who, curiously, are at odds with each other. Balgobin, the father, represents a traditional Indo-Trinidadian peasant sensibility; Romesh, the son, embodies a progressive world-view, moving from cane-field to university to working for the management of the sugar company. Both Balgobin and Romesh are ignorant of their precise propinquity, a fact known only to Seeta, Romesh's mother. Selvon uses this old literary device to allow each individual freedom to act independently. Balgobin is the exemplar of an obsolescent heroism, a heroism that recalls the conduct of the epic heroes of old. He also resembles at least one modern-day peasant hero - Santiago, the old fisherman in *The Old Man and the Sea*. Indeed a comparison between *The Plains of Caroni* and *The Old Man and the Sea* is instructive, because it reveals Selvon's intentions of writing an heroic novel. It will also, I trust, show how unfair and misguided Birbalsingh is when he assesses *The Plains of Caroni* as merely a 'collection of sketches and anecdotes jumbled together in flimsy frames of romantic intrigue'. [6]

Although *The Plains of Caroni* does not possess the parabolic intensity of *The Old Man and the Sea*, nevertheless it can be placed quite comfortably in the heroic tradition. Both Santiago and Balgobin are very old: chronologically they are the oldest men in their respective villages. They are also fortunately the oldest in experience, suffering and occupational expertise. Both are wrinkled, and exhibit the tell-tale signs of a life of hardship and industry. A juxtaposition of two descriptive passages indicates the striking similarity in experience, physical appearance, in impressive strength and in character.

> The old man was thin and gaunt with deep wrinkles in the back of his neck. The brown blotches of the benevolent skin cancer the sun brings forth from its reflection on the tropic sea were on his cheeks. The blotches ran well down the sides of his face and his hands had the deep-creased scars from handling heavy fish on the cords. But, none of the scars were fresh. They were as old as erosions in a fishless desert.
> Everything about him was old, except his eyes and they were the same color as the sea and were cheerful and undefeated. [7]

While Hemingway's parabolic intentions seem clear from the penultimate sentence, Selvon, as it were, more firmly grounds his hero:

> The fingers were long and the nails still pink and oval-shaped - an artistic hand, as they say, more suited to paint-brush or pen. The grey hairs on the back curved as if they had overlived and were curling back on their lives. But the skin stretched taut as if seeking more life, and this tautness was all over his body. Even the skin on his face had used wrinkles and creases in this quest; when he was sixty, they appeared for the first time, but gave up soon after that, and except for tiny crowsfeet and two parallel horizontal lines on his forehead - the feet from squinting in the sunlight, the lines from tension and worry - his skin was smooth. But it bore the marks of time in other ways. It was burnt a deep brown from years in the fields, and an abscess in his youth had left an ugly scar on his left forearm. [8]

Both peasant heroes, as it were, are made to represent their respective elements, the sea and the land. Santiago's destiny is on the sea: it is to catch 'the biggest fish that he had ever seen and bigger than he had ever heard of' (p45). He loves the sea in that peculiar quasi-sexual relationship that characterizes so many male responses to nature in American literature. Santiago, we are told, 'always thought of her (the sea) as feminine and as something that gave or withheld great favors, and if she did wild or wicked things it was because she could not help them' (p.20-21). Santiago is sustained by the food of the sea: the fish, the shrimp, the turtle eggs which he ate all through May to be strong in September and October, and the cup of shark-liver oil which he drank every day 'against all colds and grippes', and which is 'good for the eyes' (p.26). Passive and often supine on land, Santiago becomes the epitome of technical virtuosity and industry on sea. Balgobin, on the other hand, is a land person, more specifically, a cane man. Selvon leaves no doubt of his intention of portraying his peasant hero as a sort of embodiment of the total cane experience and process:

> His whole body oozed odour. Not the smell of sweat and dirt - these were overwhelmed by the sweet smell of molasses, and sugarcane, and rum. By smell alone, he was part of a sugar plantation. The rum had his eyes red and blood-shot, but his vision was still good. (p.10).

Both heroes fortify themselves against the ravages of time, and both are self-assured experts preparing themselves for the big fight. Both Santiago and Balgobin are men of destiny, although it is true that the sense of destiny is far more obtrusive and insistent in *The Old Man and the Sea*. Santiago is always aware of what he is and what he was born for. Balgobin is not given utterances of destiny as Santiago is, but Selvon adds a dimension to his characterization that Hemingway omits. Like Oedipus and Mr Biswas, Balgobin's fate is decreed early in his life: 'as for Balgobin, it has been decreed by the stars that he would wander and come to a sad ending' (p.11). Balgobin's heroic struggle shows him battling against fate, and his ending, although sad, is triumphant. Time and circumstance conspire to fulfil at least part of his destiny.

One fateful night, the sweet smell of cane all round them, and the silver-grey sheen of the flowers against a sky of stars, Balgobin and Seeta, his younger brother's betrothed, make love in a cane-field. Driven by 'a love that transcended all ordinary understanding', they could only 'love for the first and last time, and try, in the union to defy their destinies and capture some unforgettable togetherness to last them the rest of their lives'. Haunted by feelings similar to those Tiger feels after his violent intercourse with Doreen Robinson, Balgobin, like Cain, becomes a vagabond, and wanders 'all over the island cutting cane, ageing and disillusioned' (p.101). Through his wandering 'over the island from sugar estate to sugar estate' (pp.10-11), Balgobin unwittingly prepares himself for the fight of his life, for the battle that will immortalize his name among the villagers of Wilderness.

Santiago and Balgobin are not only associated with two occupations, but also represent a way of life. Both heroes fight desperately to preserve a way of life they believe is worth fighting for. In both novels, part of what they confront is represented by the presence of the machine. In *The Old Man and the Sea*, Santiago watches and comments on the young fishermen, 'who used buoys as floats for their lines and had motor boats', and 'on the rich with radios in their boats' (p.28). The presence of the machine is nicely adumbrated in the most ominous image of all: 'An aeroplane passed overhead on its course to Miami and he watched its shadow scaring up the schools of flying fish' (p.51). In *The Plains of Caroni*, the machine is a far more palpable and minatory presence. The mechanical harvester emerges early one morning, 'drew spangling silver across the fields', lumbering 'like some cumbersome juggernaut', with an emergency unit in attendance (p.67).

In the comparison between the mechanical harvester and 'some metal Trojan Horse' (p.68), Selvon reminds us of the most celebrated emblem of intruding treachery in classical heroic literature. The mechanical harvester represents, on the one hand, all that is inimical to the continuity of peasant life on the plains of Caroni, and on the other, the inevitable result of man's technological efforts to be more efficient and productive. Unlike Balgobin, his son Romesh, a mouthpiece for Selvon in this instance, senses the inherent ambivalence of the machine in the garden:

> there were other and more important Trinidadians who felt that with any techno-
> logical innovation, the Company was threatening the livelihood of the people. The
> bogey of the harvesting machine was the greatest threat of all. Many labourers
> looked forward to the reaping season after months of unemployment and
> hardships...But there could be no holding back or delay if the sugar industry was
> to prosper and benefit the island's economy as a whole (p.56).

Whereas Santiago, in a three-day ordeal, battles against a live fish of incredible strength and beauty, Balgobin fights a mechanical harvester, variously described as a 'lumbering cumbersome juggernaut', a 'metal Trojan Horse', a 'magic machine' (p.68) and a 'giant monster' (p.73). Such descriptive phrases serve to remind us of a literary heroic tradition, which dictates, among other things, that heroes have unique weapons, without which they cannot overcome their antagonists. Like the Red Cross Knight, Arthur and Achilles, to name a few, Balgobin, a modern epic hero, has his cutlass, affectionately called Poya, the most common Hindi term for cutlass. It is very old, sixty-years-old to be precise, with a balata handle and a steel blade whose 'fine edge was as bright as silver' (p.10). Selvon deliberately invokes the heroic tradition in his description of this venerable weapon:

> The cutlass seemed to have a life of its own. For years it had been accustomed to
> certain patterns of movement, obedient to the call of particular muscles, to a fixed
> routine of action. From the moment the hand of its master touched it, the fingers
> meshing into worn grooves on the handle. Poya knew what it had to do. If a

stranger held it, it rebelled, and once, in La Gloria, as a labourer made fun of it, it dropped from his hand and split his big toe in two, through nail and bone. Poya had longed to test itself in a variety of ways. It had descended from a strain of buccaneers; its ancestors had tasted real blood. Poya knew that several of his friends and relatives kept the buccaneering spirit alive, particularly on the banks of the Caroni, and the Indian villages...(pp.76-77).

Armed with this special weapon, with a defiant pride bordering on *hubris*, with an unshakable confidence in the rightness of his attempting to preserve the only way of life he knows, and with a profound fear of change and of the future, Balgobin engages in 'battle'. Despite the fact that Poya, somewhat like Santiago's left hand, betrays him in the ordeal, Balgobin is successful. Angry because Poya receives a six-inch 'honourable wound', Balgobin, to destroy once and for all this antagonist sent by history and progress, sets fire to the harvester:

> In the morning the combine harvester was still smouldering and smoking, but from a distance it was hardly possible to tell that anything was wrong with it. It was only on a closer look that it was discovered it had been destroyed beyond repair, still towering above the cane, but now a wreck of twisted metal (p.78).

A crucial aspect of Balgobin's heroism is his artistic potential. His right hand, we read, was 'an artistic hand...more suited to paint brush or pen' (p.10). His cutlass becomes in his expert hands a magical and artistic instrument. Its clean, clear strokes remind us of the artist's pen or brush. The artistic hand is but an external index of the inner creative spirit. Once the fateful battle is over, Balgobin, now a poet, experiences a yearning to re-enact the ordeal. In words, graphic and compelling, he recounts the battle for the moral uplift of his young nephew, Popo:

> Balgobin badly wanted to tell the story. He had lived with it, going over each little detail of the battle. He had slept with it, and in his dreams the fight was long and exhausating and he got up in the morning so tired he could hardly move (p.99).

Balgobin, therefore, like so many of Selvon's protagonists, manifests a creative desire. Tiger, Moses, Foster (*An Island Is a World*), Harry Banjo, and even Garry Johnson (*Those Who Eat the Cascadura*) are all artists inchoate; men of imagination and dedication, each succeeding, in varying degrees, to use the words of *The Plains of Caroni*, to create his personal 'glorious episode of history' (p.100).

One of the most affecting aspects of *The Old Man and The Sea* and *The Plains of Caroni* is the relationship between the hero and what we might call his heir apparent. The relationship is one of mutual love and caring. Manolin, Santiago's disciple, longs to know everything that his master can teach: 'You must get well fast for there is much that I can learn and you can teach me everything' (p.91). Similarly, Popo wants to learn as much as he can about his uncle and about cane cutting, and to this end he emulates his uncle: 'And when he got to be an old man, he was going to be like his Uncle Balgobin' (p.43). He is the young initiate, the only one allowed, as it were, in the magic circle, and 'the only one privileged to touch Poya' (p.45). Popo is taught to hold, respect and use this unique weapon:

> 'How much time I got to tell you, don't hold a cutlass with the edge turn to you?' Balgobin glowered at Popo. 'Sorry, Uncle.' The boy turned the blade.
> 'All right.' Balgobin got up. 'Now show me what you do when you face that patch of cane.'
> 'I do so, and so'. With the words the boy stepped forward and the blade was a blur as he cut the imaginary stalk of cane - two strokes at the top, one at the roots.
> 'You lie. That ain't what I teach you.' Balgobin took the cutlass. 'When you do so and so', he imitated the boy, 'you only get two cane plants. But when you do so, so, and so, and then so' - the cutlass flashed faster than the boy could follow - 'you get three cane plants, and you have your ripe cane cut, and you ready to tackle the next one' (p.45).

This, of course, is necessary training for the inevitable 'one day', when the heir apparent, turned hero, faces his true test. Both boys, as part of their complete education for their destiny, sustain the older men, spiritually and physically. Both are chosen to bring food to their mentors, who live in the humblest of abodes. Santiago lives in a shack made of the tough budshields of the royal palm, furnished with a bed, a table and a chair, and a place on the dirt floor to cook with charcoal. Balgobin's dwelling is even humbler: a hut made of the branches of the carat palm, 'with the bare necessities', no furniture, but a 'shaky table and sugar sacks' for a bed (p.104).

Unlike younger heroes, Santiago and Balgobin are old men, trying desperately to rationalize their lives, and to preserve intact a quintessential but obsolescent way of life. While the traditional epic hero is almost always forward-looking and future-oriented, these two men attempt to hold back the hands of time. But even in their retrograde struggle, they are allowed to act courageously, to stand out from the mass of mankind, and to establish a mode of conduct worthy of emulation. Santiago lives to fish another day, but his substantive role is now to teach Manolin as much as he can in his remaining years. Balgobin, however, dies after being comatose for two days, 'during which there was a great uproar throughout the length and breadth of the island'. Significantly, his death, like his life, affords him the opportunity to be heroic:

Unionists were about the only ones working overtime, rallying their party members to the cause of the downtrodden, oppressed sugar workers, calling for an end to the white imperialists and for local capital to take over, demanding that the Company withdraw all charges against the one ailing poor old man at death's door who had the courage to fight single-handed against the disaster of mechanization...Sugar workers from all over the island came to Wilderness and

formed a protecting force around the house, threatening blood and sand if any
move was made to arrest their hero (p.136-37).

With Balgobin's ashes scattered into the Caroni River, he becomes an
eternal part of the landscape and the river, so closely associated with the
moods and feelings of the people who lived near to it (p.136). In time
Balgobin's heroic life-story will no doubt become part of the 'Indian
music [the Caroni River] would learn from the farmers and cane workers
who live along its banks' (p.1). As Balgobin fought to ensure the
continuity of peasant life on the plains of Caroni, so in turn the very
peasants will ensure the perpetuity of Balgobin's indomitable struggle to
give his people their own 'glorious episode of history' (p.100).

The Plains of Caroni ends with Romesh on the verge of leaving Trinidad
for England on a Sugar Company scholarship. With Balgobin dead, the
future of the sugar industry is in his hands, and so is the future of the
Indo-Trinidadian peasantry who have tirelessly and successfully
worked the sugar-cane fields since they first came to Trinidad. It is true
that Romesh once cut cane, but nothing we know about him, except
perhaps his name, indicates that he is distinctively peasant or Indian.
His university education has forever taken him out of the cane-field, and
evidently away from traditional Indian ways. His feelings at Balgobin's
cremation seem far more removed from the expected ethnic response;
and he does not have the abiding sense of family we have come to
associate both in real life and in fiction with Indians. Furthermore, he
chooses as lover, and possibly future wife, a pretty, university-educated
local white girl, who seems as free from racial prejudice as Romesh is.
Selvon does not give Romesh an option in love, because he does not
present an Indo-Trinidadian alternative to Petra Wharton. To be fair to
Romesh, although his feelings for Petra seem genuine, his involvement
with her is at least partially to avoid any further entanglement in a
suspiciously unnatural relationship with Seeta, his young, attractive and
ambitious mother.

With his education, his dedication to research and his orientation to
the future, Romesh comes to symbolize the process by which the Indo-
Trinidadian peasant leaves the cane-field forever. Similarly, Balgobin
represents the passing of the golden era when heroic individual effort
was possible and necessary. History catches up with him, permitting
him one last heroic gasp before the incipient demise of peasant labour.
The ominous mechanical harvester, capable of doing the work of 'eighty-
eight men' (p.68), will in time totally supplant the Indo-Trinidadian
peasant, whose blood, sweat and tears have produced cane. The interests
of Industry have devalued, if not destroyed, the interest in the worker.
Although the mechanical harvester wins the war, Balgobin, in fighting
the good fight, realizes his human potential. Created both unique and
representative of his community, he becomes the apotheosis of the Indo-

Trinidadian peasant, forced by history and ethnicity to sacrifice everything to the creation of the sugar industry, which in turn sacrifices him to the 'cumbersome juggernaut' of technological innovation.

NOTES

1. Peter Nazareth, 'Interview with Samuel Selvon', in *Critical Perspectives on Sam Selvon*, ed. Susheila Nasta (Washington : Three Continents Press),1988), p.81, (hereafter cited as *Perspectives*).
2. Kenneth Ramchand, Introduction, *The Lonely Londoners* (London, 1986), p.18.
3. V.S. Naipaul, 'Turn Again Tiger', in *Perspectives*, p.123.
4. Sandra Pouchet Paquet, Introduction, *Turn Again Tiger* (London : Heinemann, 1979). pxviii.
5. Andrew Salkey, 'Plains of Caroni', in *Perspectives*, p.128.
6. Frank Birbalsingh, 'Samuel Selvon and the West Indian Literary Renaissance', in *Perspectives*, p.155-56.
7. Ernest Hemmingway, *The Old Man and the Sea* (London, 1984).
8. *The Plains of Caroni* (Toronto : Williams-Wallace 1985), p.10.

Sam Selvon: Interview with Reed Dasenbrock and Feroza Jussawalla

Reed Dasenbrock *You've been living in Canada now for some years.*

Sam Selvon: Yes, I moved in 1978, and I've been in Canada now about ten years.

RD: *Why Canada?*

Selvon: I came to England in 1950, and I spent twenty-eight years of my life here which I consider to be a good slice of my life. I suddenly felt that I had had enough of English tradition and European culture. I wanted to get back to the West before it was too late. Everyone asks why I selected Canada. Some of my wife's relatives who had settled there some years ago were doing pretty well for themselves, so she said,'let's go to Canada,' and that's how I ended up there.

RD: *Did you think at all of going back to Trinidad instead of moving to Canada? I'm thinking of* **Moses Migrating** *in which Moses thinks about returning to Trinidad but finally returns only for a holiday. Were those your sentiments as well?*

Selvon: Well, I go back from time to time. In fact, I've just been down there for three months at the beginning of this year. But I feel that I do as much for the island and for the people by living abroad, as I would be able to accomplish if I went back. I don't see that there is going to be any useful purpose being served by my returning for good. I go back from time to time and teach, but the way I see it is that I would just feel myself to be somewhat retired and off the scene if I went back to Trinidad.

RD: *You're part of a group of West Indian writers who are roughly contemporary, George Lamming, V. S. Naipaul and others, all of whom began writing in the 1950s and quickly became well known. In 1960, West Indian writing was certainly much better known than African writing in English or Indian writing in English because of these writers. Yet today, I think, one would have to say the opposite was true. Soyinka has won the Nobel prize, one reads a great deal about Achebe and Rushdie, etc. What's the difference?* (Since this interview took place Derek Walcott has won the Nobel prize and writers of the status of Caryl Phillips, John Agard, David Dabydeen, Grace Nicols, Olive Senior, Erna Brodber and many more can not be ignored, Anna Rutherford. ed.)

Selvon: I don't know. I think that there has really been a lull in literary activity, if you like, in the Caribbean since that surge, since that time of which you speak. Certainly, I don't think that there have been very many new writers since that time. Perhaps there ought to be more.

RD: *Is there a missing next generation?*

Selvon: I think so. There are some writers, for instance, who are about to reestablish themselves and have gone back and stayed in their island. In Trinidad, there's Michael Anthony and there's Earl Lovelace who both reside there. My feeling is that the new writing will have to come from the new generation rather than from the older ones like myself. That is where the surge will have to come in. It isn't that I haven't got more to write, but I just feel that is the direction from which this new movement will come.

FJ: *And yet you're very avant-garde in your own writing style. You use a kind of nativized English or local English, West Indian English, in a way no one did before you. Can you comment on the ways in which you use English? How realistic is it? How much of the style is made up of realistic cadences you're catching and how much of it is creative variance?*

Selvon: I think it's a bit of both. I really try to keep the essence, the music of the dialect. I've tried very hard to keep that. I don't do any phonetic spelling, and I try to avoid some words or phrases which I feel would be very difficult for an audience outside of the Caribbean to follow. Or if I do use it, I would try to make it clear in the text.

RD: *Can you give an example of something you might avoid?*

Selvon: Well, for instance, there's phrase that I use that has been criticized as not coming from the true dialect. The phrase is 'monkey smoke your pipe.' That's a phrase that I use; in fact, the Trinidadian phrase is, 'Crapu smoke your pipe.' Now you're going to ask me what a craptu is, I'm sure. Do you know what it is? It's a kind of frog; it's a toad. It's in the dictionary, but that's a Trinidad word. Now, I think that 'monkey smoke your pipe' has a more universal appeal and brings a good visual image to the reader much more than 'Crapu smoke your pipe.' That is definitely going to throw off the reader, immediately. However, it wouldn't throw a Trinidadian, who would say,'ah, yes, that's the real thing."

RD: *So there you would need a footnote or something like that to make it clear.*

Selvon: Exactly, and I don't like using footnotes. I like it to be all in the text of the writing. So that's a small example. Even when I began to use the word 'lime', to go'liming about,' I try to make it clear in the text that it just meant passing time away standing at a corner and watching the girls go by.

RD: *So on the one hand you try to be as accurate as possible, but on the other hand you keep at least one eye on the reader who would not understand.*

Selvon: Exactly, on the reader who might have difficulty in understanding fully. And as I say, I think that is responsible for the success that has happened. In fact, a great many other writers are now seeing that this is a form that could be used well.

RD: *Do you see your work as an influence, let's say, on Earl Lovelace in **The Dragon Can't Dance** or on other younger writers using dialect?*

Selvon: I think so. I think that children of the new generation in the schools in particular, when they are trying to write dialect now, follow that pattern by avoiding, for one thing, phonetic spelling. What I have also done with the dialect is that I have kept to standard English where I felt that it just wasn't necessary to change even the spelling of a word or anything like that. I didn't use d-e for t-h-e; I feel that t-h-e is fine with me. When I open a book, I look at a sentence, I look at the writing of it, and I say that's ok if the rhythm of dialect is still there. I feel that writing in phonetics jars the reader. I've heard many people say that reading different dialects with phonetic spelling is a bit irritating, having to analyze it all in your mind.

FJ: *One thing Wilson Harris has said to us about your work is that you've made the dialect part of the consciousness of the narrator which he doesn't do. He admires you for that. He moves from standard English to dialect only in dialogue, as opposed to having it be the consciousness of the narrator.*

Selvon: I think that those are the parts that have really shown the extent to which one can use that kind of language. If it were relegated only to dialogue, then I don't think you would see the potential. But with the narrator using dialect you can see it a little more.

RD: *It seems that the novels with Moses as the protagonist all are written almost entirely in what we've been discussing -- dialect. But some of your other novels go back and forth a little bit more. In **A Brighter Sun**, for instance.*

Selvon: Oh yes, that wasn't my style with all my work. When I started to write, at that stage it wasn't my aim to try and do something with the dialect language at all. In fact, from my earlier work up to *The Lonely Londoners* and even after *The Lonely Londoners*, I have written works like *The Plains of Caroni* using both standard English and the dialect form. I started out like most of the other writers, using the dialect form in the dialogue only. Maybe there was even a slight bit of dialect in the narrative with the first novel, but I wasn't quite conscious of it there. Some people have pointed that out to me and said: 'But look, even in your first novel you were using that dialect form in some of the narration itself.' When I looked at it, I had to agree, but that must have been really something unconscious that happened during the process of creation, because I wasn't aware of it then.

RD: *You were in a sense working towards the later works?*

Selvon: I don't know, I think I would have continued to write in both standard English and using the dialect form mainly with dialogue. It was only that when I started to write that particular novel, *The Lonely Londoners*, I just could not do it with standard English. Suddenly when I started to use 'nation language,' the Trinidad form of English, I just got on the right vehicle. It shot along and in six months the whole book was finished. It just wrote itself. It just seemed as if one was waiting for the other, as it were, and as soon as they matched, it took off.

FJ: *So you were not consciously trying to create a style or consciously trying to create a language, but writing in what was out of your consciousness.*

Selvon: That's quite true, though it's developed into something else now, in the sense that having had that earlier success, I went on to push it even more in *Moses Ascending*, where I used that same dialect form together with a kind of English dialect of its time. I merged them and used them, I think, to great effect in that particular novel. Again, the reception of the novel was mainly about the language, what has happened with the language.

RD: *Moses Ascending seems a little different in the sense that Moses himself uses a broad range of English. He moves from dialect to a very almost literary, almost Shakespearean kind of language. So his linguistic range seems enormous and then you follow him where he goes linguistically.*

Selvon: But this was the aspect I wanted to show with the Trinidad dialect. That one would work with the other. Moses's flowery language is a great deal of his pretension. The book is a satire but a lot of people are still making mistakes and not interpreting my character quite properly. Moses is a very strange, ambivalent figure, and he can't be pinned down at all. He's almost an Anansi spider character. I used him very much as I wanted to, sometimes expressing my own feelings, but sometimes he himself would take over in the process of writing the novel. There are actually sections of the book that some people feel offended by for no reason at all, because the whole thing as I say is a satire.

RD: *They identify you with Moses.*

Selvon: Yes. That may be true in some instance; I don't suppose any writer could deny that part of himself gets expressed. But not always. Sometimes Moses is there, sometimes I get into Moses, so it's a two-way thing that's going on there all the time.

FJ: *When you started to experiment with style, were you conscious of a tradition before you? Were you thinking,'I'm working in the tradition of James Joyce' or* *someone else who had been experimenting with style, or you just did this on your own as an expression of the consciousness that you were trying to depict?*

Selvon: I did this on my own. I admit to being what one would perhaps call a primitive writer, as you talk about a primitive painter, someone who does something out of some natural instinct. I've never studied the novel or studied the short story. I did a great deal of reading. I read everything I could bring my hands on from the time I was able to read, and when I started to write, I just started to write short stories. When I moved on to novels, most of my novels began as short stories and then they developed further along.

FJ: *So you didn't see yourself as coming out of a certain literary tradition?*

Selvon: No, not really. I paid very little respect to the rules, purely because I'm ignorant of them. Intuitively I found that if I was succeeding by my primitive way, I would continue to use it. That way, I also feel that I do maintain some kind of individuality in my work. For me the best pleasure I get out of writing is for someone to be able to say that that's a Selvon novel or that's a Selvon short story. I've always felt that if I probed too deeply and started to become knowledgeable about what the novel is, I would lose that individuality. Whether it is good or bad-that's something else. I've decided, because I have succeeded, that I'm going to just stay the way I am - I'll be ignorant of all these things. So I really don't think of form. I don't start without any idea, I don't sit down and wait for the muse to come to me. I do have a concept, and I do try, of course, to tie up loose ends or to round off my concept and so on, but most of the writing happens during the actual process of creation.

RD: *Do you think that others writers can get too conscious of the rules or a certain tradition, which makes their writing overly intellectual?*

Selvon: I don't know. Sometimes I feel I am the freak because I work so differently from other people. I really do. I don't conform to those things, and this is why I feel that to keep my individuality, I have to maintain a certain amount of deliberate unattachment to too many literary things. I actually teach creative writing, but I do it in my own way, with things I like. I tell my students that you can't teach writing. There are hundreds and hundreds of books that they can read that might help them, but I'm not going to help them that way. I'm just going to assist them - I can do that. I know what is good writing and what is bad writing. I've been writing long enough to know that.

FJ: *Do you think the reception of your books has somehow been conditioned by that literary environment? Do you think that you were seen as just another step, maybe, in this innovative writing technique style, or do you think it's the characters that go out and grab the reader? I know that for my own point of view, it's the characters, because you bring the characters so much alive. I find* *myself at some points very sympathetic, at some points laughing out loud responding to the characters. But I wonder if you think the English reception of the books may be conditioned because its another step in stylistic experimentation?*

Selvon: I don't know. I suppose it could partly be that too. Also, of course, there was the whole feeling that this was an exotic literature that had sprung up in the early fifties, and that it would not last. But it has not only lasted, because of the spate of books written during that time, it has actually been part of building the whole Caribbean literary tradition. I feel that I still have novels to write. I still feel I haven't written my best novel, my best book, and what I'm working on now I hope will be better than all the rest.

RD: *Can you say a little about that, or would you rather not talk about it?*

Selvon: I keep talking about it so much, and it's been delayed because I write slowly, but certainly it's a very ambitious book. I want to explore the psyche of the Caribbean mind, and to find out if in fact the West Indians have not accomplished very much and are not capable of accomplishing much, as some people say. I want to explore why that is so, if in fact it is so.

RD: *You're responding to Naipaul's famous remark, 'Nothing was created in the West Indies.'*

Selvon: Naipaul is pretty outright about it, but there are a lot of people who feel that we are not creative enough, we are indolent, and we just don't seem to care as much about literature and the fine arts. We're just happy-go-lucky kind of people, and I want to get to the psyche behind all this. I want to really explore why, if it's because of the mixture of races there or what. It's a very ambitious novel, and I know what I want to do, but it isn't easy to sit and do it.

FJ: *But you reinforce some of those stereotypes a little bit. I always remember Moses criticizing Cap in* **The Lonely Londoners**, *so that might even be you criticizing the West Indian consciousness. What is the consciousness of the West Indian man? What would you say?*

Selvon: Well, I don't know. This is what I'm really going into. I think it's a creative one. I have hopes for it. This is what I'm going to try to find out in this novel that I'm working on.

RD: *You mention the mixture of races in the West Indies. Certainly one of the things one notices about the Moses books is that, of course, Moses is black, and you are of East Indian descent. Have you been criticized for that?*

Selvon: No, not at all. In fact, I think that I am representative of what I always say is a third race in Trinidad. We talk about the blacks and the Indians being the two races there. But there is a third race who are people from my generation who grew up Westernized, who still remain what they are because you can't change yourself, but who have adopted a way of life which tries to work and operate between the two races and who are Creolized as it were, and who see themselves more as West Indians than as perhaps belonging to people who originally came from India.

FJ: *And they also see themselves more Westernized.*

Selvon: They are more Westernized and they are creating a nation out of this mixture. I'm not the only one. Very few people talk about that third race, but that is a race that exists. I know that it exists, and that is the race that I am putting my hopes on for any future for Trinidad.

RD: *So as opposed to those people who would see themselves first as black or first as Indian, there are other people who would see themselves first as West Indian or Trinidadian. How does your work express that?*

Selvon: I think I've always tried to keep an element of that in my work. I've always tried to give more voice to this publicly in many ways, whenever I talk, wherever I go. Even from the first novel, from *A Brighter Sun*, I've been concerned with the existence of these races that could live in some kind of workable harmony.

RD: *Like the friendship between Tiger and Joe.*

Selvon: Yes. It's something that people know about. If that never existed, a lot of people would have criticized the book to hell. But people of my generation know that kind of living together happened, actually existed and still exists to some extent in Trinidad.

FJ: *That's similar to the whole generation here now both in England and maybe even in America of the children of immigrants from Asia and the West Indies. So, for instance, there's the Asian writer here, Hanif Kureishi, who really should be British because he's part British and Pakistani, yet that generation seems to be less accepted by the white establishment than the purer West Indian or the purer East Asian generation. It's an interesting comment to me that this generation which is by birthright British or American is less accepted than the immigrant generation.*

Selvon: I imagine that there are very, very interesting aspects about that new generation that you talk about that I am hoping will come out. I would hope very much that the new writing will come out of that generation already. I know that there's been a considerable amount of short story writing and poetry and so on. I am hoping that there will be one of two big novels coming out from that new generation that will depict their times and experiences as *The Lonely Londoners* did for the fifties and sixties.

FJ: *I wonder what happens to the consciousness of this generation. I've been*

thinking about this a lot just because I just finished reading V.S. Naipaul's
Enigma of Arrival. It's interesting in the way in which that book is both Hindu
- gives expression to his Hindu consciousness - and yet wants not to be. I wonder
if this forthcoming generation will then also be like a Naipaul consciousness that
says, 'No, we're not really what we came from; we don't want to be associated
with it; we want to be white, mainstreamed.'

Selvon: I don't know. That would be very interesting to see. I think that
this is a kind of dilemma that doesn't face just one individual. I think it's
a dilemma that faces any number of people who move out of one culture
into another, particularly people from Third World countries because of
their color, who move into white societies to settle. And I think that they
have this problem of how they are going to identify themselves. Are they
going to keep their original identity or keep their roots, or are they going
to allow themselves to be assimilated completely into their new culture?

RD: *Is it different in Canada? Is the dynamic different in Canada and Britain?*

Selvon: No, there is no difference in this particular point that I was just
making. The difference that does exist is that West Indians who are
westernized get along much easier, I think, in a place like Canada than
they do when they come to England. English culture is so much more
stiff upperlip and closed which they're not quite accustomed to. There
has always been a fairly easy going relationship between the Americas
and the Caribbean - we are part of the same area. We practically come
under American politics, some are already somewhat Americanized in
the Caribbean.

FJ: *Should these people make some effort to retain either their Caribbean selves*
or Indian selves or African selves, or should they seek to mainstream themselves
rather than to retain their identity? If they did this, would it just generate a kind
of robotic culture, a culture without culture, as it were?

Selvon: I don't know. It could evolve a new culture for that matter. If you
say a culture without a culture, that is a kind of culture. *(Laughter)*
However the dilemma would be resolved, I would certainly feel that they
should not forget their past, their background, where they come from. I
have always remained Trinidanian myself. I know where I come from,
and I know that by race I am mixed. I am predominately East Indian, I
know that, but that doesn't stop me from formulating my own
philosophy or my own psychological approach as to how I am going to
assimilate myself into the culture. I don't know which is best, but I
would certainly hope that they would not forget their past or turn a blind
eye to the origins of the whole thing. I don't think that you can build a
future without using the past, and I don't think that they should try to
forget their origins at all. But certainly I think they should make some
effort to assimilate into the society in which they have to live day by day.

Are we going to have just ghettos of people who are living completely apart?

RD: *Of course, if the East Indians had done that in Trinidad, you wouldn't have the third race that you're talking about.*

Selvon: Exactly, you see, so that's not integrating at all.

FJ: *What is the reception of the East Indians in the West Indies? Have they integrated themselves within the fabric of society or are they, as I see here in London, in almost separate townships, as it were.*

Selvon: I think that it's about half and half. There are people, like myself, my generation, who have been Westernized. Then there are others who have remained more Indian.

RD: *Is that true of the writers too do you think?*

Selvon: I've never studied the writings of the writers to that extent, but I am pretty sure that probably you would get elements of that existing in the writers as well.

RD: *George Lamming many years ago in* **The Pleasures of Exile** *praised you at the expense of Naipaul because he said that you were exceptional among West Indian writers for being willing to deal with the multi-racial situation.*

Selvon: Well, it's true; what else have I got to deal with? That is the problem that we have. So, you know, I can't turn a blind eye to it. In fact, the thing with me is that I am so much Westernized, so much Creolized, that it's the only element that I think that I am really strongest in. In some of my books, I've tried to avoid going into too much description of Indian ritual and custom purely because I don't know them myself.

FJ: *Could I ask, are you from a Tamil background? The name Selvon sounds Tamil.*

Selvon: I think so, I think perhaps it could be from a Tamil background. I've never really tried tracing it back, but I have a feeling that it might well be from the south of India.

FJ: *How many generations does that go back?*

Selvon: I would be third; I guess about two generations back.

RD: *Your grandfather came from India? And you were brought up in a completely English-speaking environment?*

Selvon: Yes. That's right, yes, from the time I was small. My mother could speak Hindi very well.

FJ: *Your mother was half-Indian?*

Selvon: Yes, my mother's father was Scottish, and her mother was

Indian.

RD: *So then you were probably brought up in a more Creolized society than Naipaul.*

Selvon: I would definitely say so. From the time I was small, it's what I knew. And yet, as I say, you can't forget who you are. I had aunts and uncles living in the country districts who were really what's called the orthodox Indians. I would go there and they would wear saris and cook roti, and so on, so I think I had a good taste of both.

FJ: *So you yourself are a kind of multicultural consciousness. You grew up with that kind of multicultural consciousness.*

Selvon: Exactly, you see. A lot of my friends in my neighbourhood and in my school in the town that I grew up in were mixed blacks and Indians.

RD: *You grew up in Port of Spain?*

Selvon: In San Fernando. it's the second largest city in Trinidad after Port of Spain.

RD: *Therefore what you're talking about in terms of this third race is very much what was being created when you were growing up.*

Selvon: Yes, and as I say, I know this from people of my generation. I have to admit my Indian blood, what I am, but certainly I think of myself more as a West indian. Perhaps I even want to go further than that and create a Caribbean mind, one who comes out of that particular part of the world.

RD: *What's the difference there between West Indian and Caribbean?*

Selvon: I was going to say Trinidadian, but even with West Indian there would be a difference. I prefer the word Caribbean. I like it; it's a nicer word. I think that people tend to make mistakes about what is a West Indian. People here in England hear the terms West Indian and they say,'You're from West India?' they don't know.

RD: *Let me go on a little bit with this Trinidad question. You're saying that you prefer to move beyond a kind of local consciousness to a larger area.*

Selvon: Yes

RD: *But of course the Caribbean is not just English speaking; it is also French speaking and Spanish speaking. Does this change as you move from an English-speaking milieu?*

Selvon: Yes, I think it will change, but we will just have to say the English-speaking Caribbean in that sense. We would have to move first to, say, an English-speaking Carribean consciousness, and then extend it to incorporate the French and the Dutch and the Spanish and so on. The Spanish do that. They're incorporating the English-speaking Caribbean with their arts festivals and things like that in Cuba and drawing them in. So I think we also should be doing some of that sort of thing. But we should bring them to us rather than we go to them.

RD: *What are the advantages of that? What if someone said: 'I'm from Trinidad, I don't know what the Caribbean is,' what would you say to that?*

Selvon: Well, I think it's more likely that they'll know where the Caribbean is, but they don't know where Trinidad is. I think it'll work that way. I think that the concept is a bigger one. People in England all know where the Caribbean is, but they can't identify what island is in it. They don't know where Trinidad is. It is also a much more ambitious concept to try and get a national feeling among the English-speaking Caribbean writers. This is not just my dream because they've tried it already with the Federation in the late forties. I myself was very disappointed when that fell through.

RD: *Why do you think it broke down?*

Selvon: Well, I think it's just because we couldn't agree among ourselves. There was all this bickering. Trinidad feels that it's a better island than Jamaica, and Jamaica feels it's the biggest English-speaking island. They want everything to happen over there, and Barbados doesn't want to have anything to do with it. That sort of petty rivalry that goes on has been keeping us apart for years and years. I think we are slowly growing out of that now, and we are able, at least, to get together and talk more about what will be done for the area as a whole. In fact, it is already, in a way, in practice with trade agreements going on between the islands and so on.

RD: *But you're saying there's a cultural component?*

Sevlon: The cultural thing is what has to follow now. It should really be going side by side, but culture, of course, is the best thing in the budget of any Caribbean government.

RD: *It may be, in a sense, easier for you in Canada or a writer in England to have that regional sense that you're talking about than someone in the area, because they may have more of a sense of the differences between the islands.*

Selvon: I quite agree with you. Most Caribbean people who have moved out of the islands and settled abroad have really established themselves well, not only as writers, not only in the field of art and so on, but in other professions and in medicine and social work. Any part of the English-speaking world you go to you can see these West Indians in very responsible seats, you know, very high administrative levels they're working in all over. I feel that this is a very good thing for the Caribbean.

I think that this is why the rest of the world has become interested in the Caribbean.

FJ: *Because it breaks the 'stereotypes'?*

Selvon: Yes. Who are these people? They've got these writers - what's it like down there? This is why people become interested. So I think they do a good job; I think we do a good job. We're not really exiles in that sense.

RD: *Ambassadors perhaps.*

Selvon: Yes.

RD: *Therefore, maybe this broader consciousness will come largely from this community abroad.*

Selvon: I think so. When I talk to West Indians who are living abroad about it, they sense it much more than back home. When I first came to England in the fifties, for the first time I met people from all the other islands that I had never met before in Trinidad. For the first time in my life, I was meeting Grenadians, Jamaicans, Barbadians - four thousand miles away from the Caribbean, here in the heart of London meeting these people from the other islands that I'd never seen in my life before.

FJ: *So your new Caribbean consciousness, the man with the new Caribbean consciousness, would blend all these as well as the immigrant consciousness?*

Selvon: I would hope so. What I would like to see being done further is I would like to see writers writing about movement from one island to the other. I don't really want a novel about Trinidad. I want the characters to move and go up to UWI [University of the West Indies] in Jamaica and spend a week in Barbados - have friends in Barbados, have friends in Cuba. This is what I'm hoping to do in the new novel.

FJ: *That's a good note to end on, and we'll await your book then, in a couple of years or a year you think?*

Selvon: I hope it'll be a year. It's a very ambitious project, as I'm sure you appreciate, but I hope it will be a year.

SAM SELVON

A Special Preface by Moses Aloetta Esq. (1991)

It have a lot of myths and legends and nancy stories that circulate since I, Moses Aloetta Esq., presented my credentials to the literary world. Some people think I am an arsehole, some people say I am an enigma that never arrived, the chosen few consider me a genius, and one evening at a big literary conference at the Commonwealth Institute in London whilst I was reading a bawdy passage from one of my tomes in front of a big audience that included *Whites* a black Guyanese bitch walked up to the microphone and slap me bam bam in my face. I wouldn't of minded if *Blacks* alone was present, but to slap me in front of White people really hurt.

The author has often been asked how much of the books is himself, or the fictional character, or the actual person who inspired him. In the process of creativity, unknowingness is the quintessence that propels me - I want to know as much as the reader what happens next, or what shit 'Moses' is going to come out with, and when I emerge, your guess is as good as mines as to who is the culprit. So that when literary critics - seeing some significance in the name as the biblical Moses who led his people out of bondage - as me, 'were you thinking of that when you were writing about your Moses and the black immigrants settling in England'. I can only say. 'no, the name is common in Trinidad, and I, just pull it out of a hat.' But they dig and delve. Look for plot and sub-plot. Climax and anti-climax, purpose and motive. The machinations that went on in my mind whilst I was writing, if I had them all the time I would be writing books like peas.

Of the factual human being that Moses was based upon, I know that under the welter of adversity, and the wonderment of living in the heart of the Mother Country after coming from a small island known only to map-readers, was the yearning to be a writer. 'Boy,' he told me, 'is as if I only start to live since I come to Brit'n. I wish I was a writer like you.' Instead, he was a master raconteur. Not that he held forth recounting the ballads and episodes: he would drop a hint or a clue and leave it up to his listeners to embellish or elaborate. His word-to-the-wise economy sometimes exasperated me, and I would ask, 'but what actually happen?' and he would shrug and say, 'imagine if you was me...what you would of done?'

I did nothing about writing down his adventures until I got the 'distant perspective' from a writers' colony in the United States. I started to make notes, and when I returned to England I sat down to write *The Lonely Londoners*. I couldn't make any headway; was totally frustrated until I realised I was using the wrong kind of right English. I tried the 'nation language' of the English-speaking Caribbean and everything fell smoothly into place. I made some slight modifications, mainly by not spelling phonetically or shifting a phrase to make it more understandable. Some diehard Caribbean critics claimed that it lost authenticity.

Be that as it may, the book was highly praised in England and the United States, special reference made to 'the injection of new blood into the English language.'

Some twenty five years went by before Moses appeared again *(Moses Ascending)* to depict the changes during that time-a new generation of Black Britons, and an influx of Indians and Pakistanis had come to add *more* colour to the scene. Moses has ascended to being a landlord, and his language has escalated from the basement to the penthouse, a kind of hybrid mixture of ye-olde and what-happening. Once again the language swept the book along like a cork on a tidal wave, and the critics were full of praise.

In fact, though I had not anticipated doing another book on the life and adventures of Moses, I was in high gear. As it happened, the true-true Moses felt that Brit'n had taken its toll not only on his philosophy but his physiology, and he decided to peter out his days in the warmth of the tropic sun in his homeland of Trinidad.

I well remember some faithful friends saw him off at Waterloo Station, in good time to catch the boat-train. This was where it had started, and this was where it was going to end as far as his life in London was concerned. There were no tight throats, no gruff voices, no loose-fingered hand raised surreptitiously to wipe away a tear. We covered sentiment with banter and old-talk, recalling the old days, joking about how he would miss scouting the streets of London to pick up a sleeper. Finally, we all shook hands and embraced him. And he left London.

Truth is *stronger* than fiction. Who knows what ballads and episodes more graphic and pertinent that any I have tried to describe in the books he might have taken away to reminisce over in his rocking-chair days?

He might well have rested in peace had I not decided to follow him to Trinidad in the present novel *Moses Migrating*. And considering the characteristics that are his trademark - the mimicry, the convolutions of irony and satire, the ambivalences - nothing seemed more appropriate than the celebration of Carnival, a national, emotional event that is more important to the people than voting for Prime Minister or taking precaution against a devastating hurricane. Somewhere between the actuality and the dreamworld of fiction the truth about Moses-the truth about the whitewashed Black man torn apart by the circumstances of living in a white society-exists. If I as author consciously strived at anything when he gave me a chance, it was to keep some thread of authentic commentary of the tribulations of Black people surviving away from their roots, which I tried to weave into the kiff-kiff laughter: there is no question that Britain's image needed a boost at the time of his migration: there is no question that *any* Black immigrant returning to his homeland would have qualms about resettling.

The humour and entertainment that Moses provides sometimes tend to overwhelm the serious side of his nature. It is a knack that all Black people acquire to survive. In my own years in London, any hardcore material I wrote about Blacks had to have ha-ha.

So laugh your guts out. But remember there is more in the mortar than the pestle.

An Afterword on Moses's Preface

The Preface above, which Sam wrote in 1991 for the publication of an American edition of *Moses Migrating* which was originally published in Britain in 1983, marks an important moment in Caribbean literary history and refers to an episode which occurred during a conference on Caribbean writing held at the Commonwealth Institute in London in the autumn of 1986. Sam was present as an invited guest at this conference along with many other distinguished writers including Austin Clarke, Earl Lovelace, Lorna Goodison, Martin Carter, Grace Nichols, John Agard, James Berry to name but a few. Whilst reading a satirical extract from *Moses Ascending* (1975) Sam was slapped across the face by a black Guyanese woman who left her seat in the audience and delivered the blow on the stage where he was standing. The offending passage (which we had discussed on route from the airport in to London) was taken from a moment in the novel where the would-be writer/narrator Moses is commenting with irony on the new generation of 'Black Britons' that were threatening to take over the city:

Blessed be the new generation of Black Britons, and blessed be I that I am still alive and well to witness their coming of age from picaninny to black beauty. It is a sight for sore eyes to see them flounce and bounce about the city, even if they capsize on their platforms and trip up in their maxis. Be it bevy or crocodile, Women's Lib or Women's Tit, they are on the march, sweeping through the streets. You see one, you see two, you see a whole batch of them. There are no woman in the world who could shake their backsides like a black woman...It may be that they inherit that proud and defiant part of their anatomy from toting and balancing loads on their heads from the days of slavery. But howsoever it come into being, it is good to look at...(pp.21-2).

Whilst the passage clearly pokes fun at black women it has to be seen in the context of the novel as a whole which is utterly subversive and satirical and targets everyone - whether white, black, male, female, fellow writers or Moses's illiterate white Man Friday from the Black Country.

It was an important moment in Caribbean literary history because not only was the man who had mythologized London for black people in *The Lonely Londoners* (1956) publicly assaulted by a black woman but also because of the effect it had on all the other writers present who, whether male or female, respected the central significance of Sam's work in the development of a Caribbean literary tradition. The woman did apologize but Sam himself was deeply wounded by the incident and talked of not reading in London again though he did come back several times in the following years. He questioned however whether his work could still be read in such a climate and he prevented me from publishing an article in the national press on the subject preferring to not make a stir. Nevertheless, he proceeded to tour the Caribbean in that very year reading the piece over and over again. The preface to *Moses Migrating* followed later.

The event has of course taken on mythological proportions in memory and many writers/critics have referred to it since but I do want to put the record straight on one thing and that is that the passage was from *Moses Ascending* not *The Lonely Londoners* as many people have suggested. The slippage is interesting: were those early black veterans of the city, the parents of today's black population being violated yet again? In a way it is not important, for Selvon's black Londoners live on and have been immortalized in the imaginations of several generations of readers and writers.

Susheila Nasta

HELEN TIFFIN

'Under the Kiff-Kiff Laughter': Stereotype and Subversion in *Moses Ascending* and *Moses Migrating*

With the possible exception of V. S. Naipaul's Mr Biswas, no other character in West Indian fiction is as well-known and well loved as Sam Selvon's Moses Aloetta. Moses is the central figure in three of Selvon's novels, and his adventures in London and Trinidad span a crucial thirty years of contemporary West Indian migration to Britain. *The Lonely Londoners* (1956) details the fortunes (and misfortunes) of Moses and his fellow West Indians in the metropolis in the early years of West Indian mass migration. By the time of *Moses Ascending* (1975) generational 'indigenisation' of West Indians in Britain, independence, and Black Power movements had altered the London scene. West Indians had gained an often uneasy foothold in 'the motherland' and Moses is now the owner of his own house, though (not untypically) his fortunes suffer a reversal at the end. *Moses Migrating* (1983) builds on this contemporary relation between a more 'indigenised' generation of West Indians and their 'ancestral' island homelands, and like many of his contemporaries and their British-born progeny, Moses returns to Trinidad for Carnival.

Without ever denying - indeed often foregrounding - colonial and post-colonial West Indian experiences of racism, poverty, marginalisation and abuse in London, Selvon, through his figurations of Moses, offers hilarious, good-humoured, complicated, healing novels of racial and colonial interaction whose radically subversive strategies are hidden 'under the kiff-kiff laughter '.

In an interview in 1979, Selvon noted that:

> The comedy element has always been there among black people from the Caribbean. It is their means of defence against the sufferings and tribulations that they have to undergo. I always felt that this is a very strong element indeed and it is too easily brushed aside by well-meaning critics who feel that the funny story has its place but it is just so much and nothing more. I think it is a great deal more.[1]

Under the 'kiff-kiff laughter' then, the purpose of Selvon's intricately ironic novels is serious. A number of critics have noted the complex tonal modalities of *The Lonely Londoners* [2] and examined the subversive strategies of *Moses Ascending*[3], But *Moses Migrating* has generally been ignored or dismissed as a lesser sequel to the 1975 novel, having little to add beyond the prolongation, into the 1980s, of the adventures of a now popular Trinidadian character.[4]

But to imply that Selvon's three 'Moses novels' constitute a trilogy is to ignore important differences between them; differences related not only to changing times, but to major shifts in tone and technique between the earlier *Lonely Londoners* and the two later works. While the former is character-centred and generally realist in mode, the later works are increasingly focussed on a more general exploration and interrogation of the role of representation in the construction of colonial subjectivities. In *Moses Ascending* and *Moses Migrating* Selvon turns to examination of racist and colonialist stereotypes and their most naturalised figure, the cliché. Consequently the later novels are more broadly satirical in mode, and Moses himself is represented as a much more extreme product of the processes of colonialist interpellation than he was in the earlier novel. And while *Moses Ascending* and *Moses Migrating* share this anatomisation of the stereotype in colonial discourse, they address the matter through rather different topoi.

In 'The Other Question' Homi Bhabha argues that a primary strategy of colonialist discourse is the circulation of the stereotype, which, through its repetitive 'fixity' renders the colonised 'knowable and visible'. Anti-colonial discourses have thus focussed on exposing the effectivity of the stereotype, on destabilising its apparent 'fixity' and on unmasking the imperialist anxieties which underlie and energise its still efficacious repetitions. But as Bhabha argues, to

> judge the stereotyped image on the basis of a prior political normativity is to dismiss it, not to displace it, which is only possible by engaging with its effectivity; with the repertoire of positions of power and resistance, domination and dependence that constructs the colonial subject (both colonisers and colonised).[5]

In *Moses Ascending* and *Moses Migrating* Selvon recirculates and reanimates racist and colonialist clichés and stereotypes, interrogating and destabilising them through partial, ironic and/or incomplete inversions of the binary codes which are foundational to both the production and the persisting potency of such stereotypic figurations. In unmasking and dismantling stereotypes of both colonisers and colonised, frequently by 'collapsing' one into the other, Selvon relies primarily on his (re)figuration of Moses in the later novels as an almost absurdly interpellated colonial subject, 'obedient' (to use Pechàux's term) to the point of caricature. The ironic distance between Selvon and Moses is thus far greater in the two later works than it is in *The Lonely Londoners*, and both texts focus more on an investigation of colonial and post-

colonial subjectivities than on presenting a 'realist' account of West
Indian experiences in London or English travellers in Trinidad.

In colonialist discourse the potency of the stereotype depends not just
on its fixity and its endless repetition but on the binaristic codifications
that serve as its inescapable foundations. Such rigidly maintained
binaries as coloniser/colonised; master/slave; white/black; 'European'/
'native' are, of course, also hierarchised. Interpellated and 'obedient'
colonial subjects like Moses represent the fulfilment of colonialist desire;
they are products of an apparently perfected imperialism which, to
borrow from Macaulay's 1835 *Indian Education Minute*, has produced
'Indians in blood and in colour, but English in taste, in opinions, in
morals and in intellect.' [6]

But this 'perfected' colonial subjectivity is inherently destabilising of
those very hierarchised binaries upon which the ideology of empire and
colonial governance rests, since paradoxically such 'ideal ' subjects
necessarily annihilate those very divisions by which their subjectivity is
constituted. Moses' taste(s), opinions, morals, intellect, (and, one might
add, affiliations and loyalties) are, he believes, white and English. But
Afro-Trinidadian in 'blood and colour' Moses' Anglo-affiliative speech
and behaviour occasionally produces a degree of self-mockery and
constantly attracts the derision of others - West Indians and Britons
alike. It is not only through Moses' split colonial subjectivity however
that Selvon interrogates stereotypes and their binary bases. In both
Moses Ascending and *Moses Migrating* comedy, irony and subversion are
enacted through a series of narrative inversions, intertextural and
historical ironies, which unsettle stereotypical figurations and the
hierarchies which provide their foundation. Characteristically however,
these inversions are never fixed or completed but produce further
inversions and upsets which energise more vortices of spiralling
instabilities.

In *Moses Ascending* the black poverty-stricken foreign 'migrant' (who is
not quite 'foreign' and has come 'home' to the motherland; and is thus
not really a 'migrant ' either) becomes landlord and resident, owner of a
'great house' in London, renting rooms to other Commonwealth
'migrants'. Man Friday thus becomes Crusoe, inverting those
paradigmatic stereotypes which were reflected in and widely dissem-
inated through Defoe's influential 1719 work. Landlord Moses takes on,
as helper/servant, the illiterate English Bob from the 'Black Country' of
the white heartland (the Midlands) of England. (And Moses resolves,
like Crusoe, 'to teach' Bob The Bible when he 'have the time'). Inversions
of the roles of master and servant; white and black; coloniser and
colonised here serve to denaturalise the stereotypes and their hierarchi-
sation; to expose their constructedness, their interested representational
foundations.

But these 'inversions' are neither neat nor completed, both because of

Moses' 'split' colonial subjectivity and because he is still in so many ways a relatively powerless black immigrant in a white country. Moses' 'house' is already condemned when he buys it. In *Moses Ascending* he thus inhabits the positions of both owner and tenant; master and servant; coloniser and colonised; black and white. At the end, in spite of his retention of the ownership of the house, he has been (re)relegated to the basement by a now literate Bob, in possession of the 'tools ' of representation, having, ironically, been taught these by Moses.

Such an interplay of ironic reversals produces wonderful comic effects and serves to erode the binarist foundations of the stereotype itself, without surrendering the novel's political purchase. (To suggest that in a post-imperial metropolitan context, the West Indian had become 'landlord' would be (if salutary) idealist and politically irresponsible). Moses is thus never really accorded status as resident and landlord in English 'society'. Though he is (as an obedient 'white') opposed to the black power ideology of Brenda and Galahad, he is the 'test ' arrested at the rally and though Moses has to teach Bob his own language, once he does so, Bob regains control and, Caliban/Friday-like, Moses is exiled to his own basement. He still owns his (slum) property in the metropolis, but it is really Bob in the penthouse who has the upper hand. Using the stereotype of the 'English gentleman ' - a figure to which Moses aspires and to which he is certainly closer than Bob - Bob is able to appeal to 'English ' morals in punishing Moses for his sexual exploits with Jeannie. In the face of all evidence to the contrary, the working class Bob, always eager to have sex with any female and constantly harrassing (black) Brenda, invokes a useful English 'stereotype' (to which he assumes himself entitled by 'race and birth' but which the novel challenges) to send a chastened Moses (more sensitive to the mythology of the English gentlemanly code) back to the basement.

But in *Moses Ascending* and *Moses Migrating* Selvon also targets that particular form of language associated with the stereotype - the cliché. In the contemporary world clichés, perhaps more than any other figurations, perpetuate the stereotype through the ways in which they have been naturalised, 'unconsciously ' absorbed into everyday speech. Selvon takes up the clichés, repeating, recycling and subversively rewriting it with spectacular comic effect: 'It does seem to a black man that though he is as pure and white as the driven snow ... it got something, somewhere, sometime, what he do wrong, and that even if it don't exist, the police would invent one to trap him'.[7] The persistent repetition (with significant variation) of clichés about both blacks and whites, as well as their interrogation and dismantling through action and dialogue in the novel is again both delightfully comic and radically subversive.

In *Moses Migrating*, fed up with his basement accommodation and his 'apple cart' (the complicated metaphoric connections between economic

status in Trinidad and London, apples, serpents, and 'having your apple
cart upset' are significant) Moses decides to return to Trinidad for an
initially unspecified period. Once again Selvon is primarily concerned
with the continuing power of stereotype and cliché and with
destabilising their binaristic bases. His technique is again broadly one of
comic/ironic spiralling inversions enacted through episodes of role-
reversal and cross-dressing, though, as in *Moses Ascending*, such
inversions are always qualified, always unstable. Moses is again figured
as the deeply interpellated colonial subject who (usually in spite of
himself) occupies both binaristic stereotypes, and so too (in a minor key)
does his English foil, Bob. While Moses is (provisionally) elevated to the
status of gentleman, master and Briton, English Bob is frequently
represented in the stereotypical roles of servant, dupe, 'savage', ill-
educated bore. (In both *Moses Ascending* and *Moses Migrating* Selvon
unpicks the 'seamless' stereotype of the white colonising Briton through
his representation of Bob and Jeannie; through Moses' experience and
knowledge of British class and regional divisions; and through contrasts
between the language of 'high' English culture and literature and
contemporary vulgar London speech). But in spite of his experience of
Bob and his detailed knowledge of the metropolis, Moses of *Moses
Migrating* still clings determinedly to the imperial stereotype, to the era
when Britannia 'ruled the waves' and her civilising missionaries could
never have succumbed to sea-sickness.

Where *Moses Ascending* focussed on the master-slave relation (and the
'mastertext' of *Robinson Crusoe*), *Moses Migrating* uses the topoi of
movement and migration to unsettle colonialist stereotypes which are
based on inflexible oppositions between race purity, ancestral lineage
and the 'mongrel'; 'native' and 'foreign'; 'home' and 'abroad'; tourist and
resident. It also addresses (both implicitly and explicitly) the
relationship between economics and empire, culture and migration and
persisting econo-cultural cliches: 'Coin of the realm'; 'two sides of the
coin'; 'streets paved with gold'; and the myth of El Dorado and the
economic disillusionment of West Indian workers in London.

Two primary motivations energised the massive colonialist migrations
of the last four centuries. Voyages of Europeans to the Caribbean were
generally motivated by the promise of economic gain and mass
migrations to Europe by the colonised (and formerly colonised) in the
twentieth century were similarly sponsored by a hope of economic
improvement. Both 'migrations ' were underpinned by two powerful
myths - the myth of El Dorado and the imperial myth of the metropolis
where streets would be 'paved with gold'.

But a second imperial mythology underlay colonial migrations to
Britain - the myth of the 'mother' country with all its implications of
welcome and affiliation which had been sponsored by the nineteenth
and twentieth century rhetoric of empire (mothers and children, sisters

and brothers) and deliberately fostered, in the twentieth century, in educational curricula. The rhetoric of 'the family' and the 'mother country' denied those racial differences upon which the ideology of empire itself rested. As the colonial 'chickens' came home to roost [8] in the imperium, however, their experience was, well, a horse of a different colour. Whiteness, Englishness, biological ancestry were what really mattered. The would-be children were received as unwelcome and uncivilised rough colonials; foreigners, not residents.

Yet these (re)turning colonials were *both* 'children' of the Empire and foreigners within it; closely related and no relation at all; black and white, their parentage both genetic (biological) *and* Anglo-representational. As Moses tells us:

> Up to this moment I have never told a soul the truth about my past, that I was born a norphan, and left to my own devices to face the wicked world, deposited on the doorsteps of a distant cousin in an old wicker basket, and nearly get tote away by the dustman and dump in the *labasse*. It was childless Tanty Flora ... who took me under her wing and gave me the name Moses ... [9]

Moses' biological ancestry may thus be rather obscure, but his cultural and representational ancestry is here exposed as a direct European lineage through fairy tales and nineteenth century accounts of infants abandoned on 'the doorstep' in wicker baskets(!) to the Biblical Moses in the bullrushes. *Moses Migrating* thus examines questions of biological and cultural allegiances; migration and ancestral origins, concepts of 'blood' and 'home'; exploration, and its contemporary manifestation, tourism, and the foreigner and 'native'.

At the beginning of *Moses Migrating* Moses has decided to return to Trinidad, and Bob and Jeannie resolve to accompany him as tourists. To prepare for this journey into the 'wilds' with their 'native informant' Moses, they purchase what they regard as appropriate clothing. Dressed as the stereotypes of the European explorer 'on safari'; they appear before Moses as representations of representations. Asked to inspect and approve these outfits, ('I don't want to go around looking like a proper Charlie,' Bob says), Moses acts like a colonel reviewing the troops. The passage is a lengthy one, but it illustrates the intricate ironic interplay of Selvon's re-citation/re-sitation of colonialist clichés and stereotypes and their radical destabilisation:

> Jeannie had on leather boots coming up to her knees, a thick furry-looking midi-skirt belted at the waist, a white cotton shirt, a colourful bandanna round she neck, and one of them cork hats like what you see film stars wear on safari. The hat was trim with mosquito-netting material, like what demure brides wear.
> Bob, standing at her side, had on heavy, black boots, white stockings up to his hairy calves, a short pair of khaki drill trousers, a safari jacket with a pipe sticking out of the top pocket, a cork hat like Jeannie but without the veil, and he was sloping arms with a great elephant gun.

Oh, and both of them were wearing giant sunglasses, so big almost covering their faces.
I did not laugh. I looked them over appraisingly. I went and do a parade inspection, straightening Bob's hat, patting and turning down the flap of the pocket over Jeannie's left breast, then I stood in front of them, frowning a little.
'Well?' Bob say.
'Assume those are your costumes for playing Carnival?' I ask.
Bob frown now. 'It's our tropical gear.'
'It might do for Port-of-Spain, ' I say, 'but when you get into the interior the natives will laugh at you. You'll have to discard all that.'
'You mean walk around starkers? ' Jeannie ask interestingly.
'I won't have that,' Bob say. 'It's okay for Moses if he wants to revert, but we have to toe the line somewhere.' [10]

Ironic treatment of the notion of reversion ('going native'), categories of explorer and indigene, resident and tourist, black and white are here subjected to ironic inversion and dissolution. (Bob, meaning that (as representative white) he will have to maintain imperial 'standards', remarks that 'we have to toe the line somewhere ' when of course he means 'draw the line'). And there is the further irony that Moses, not Bob and Jeannie (who are going as tourists, purely for pleasure), is the one with the 'civilising mission' - to set an 'example' to his countrymen and to reassure them that in spite of the decline in the value of the English pound, Britannia still 'rule the waves'.

If Moses begins the voyage - a kind of backwards sailing of the middle passage - in a third class cabin with Bob and Jeannie in first class, he nevertheless 'migrates' (on the advent of Bob's mal de mer) to the floor of the upper class cabin (with Jeannie). Allowed into this section at her behest, then taking Bob's place in 'entertaining ' her and indeed wearing Bob's clothes, he is consequently annoyed to find that Bob and Jeannie have cast him as their servant. Once again, Moses is represented by Selvon as protean, unwittingly resisting in his movements and manoeuvres during the voyage, the stereotypes which pervade the language and which still remain fundamental to the thinking of the English and West Indian passengers and to Moses himself.

As both returning 'native' and civilising explorer, Moses, on arrival in his Trinidadian 'homeland' does not rush off to Tanty Flora's house but stays at the Hilton with Bob and Jeannie, once again inhabiting both the roles of tourist and son of the soil. Moses' identification with such ostensibly antagonistic stereotypes and his comic vacillations between them is further emphasised by his discovery that the orange seller he can see from his Hilton window is not the 'picturesque' market woman beloved of the tourist, but Tanty Flora (to whom, as a foundling, he is both related and not related). Moses rushes across the road to a not-so-touching scene of reconciliation, when Tanty angrily rejects his generous offer to buy all her oranges with his English pounds. Moses is keen to represent this scene to himself however, as such scenes should be represented: 'Laugh if you want. I don't care. That's the way it happen. I may be hard-boiled and black, but tender is the night, and I am not abashed to confess that poignant moment in the sunlight' (p.64).

In ironic contrast to Moses' lack of interest in 'roots ', white 'imperialist' /tourist Bob has a personal mission in Trinidad: to trace his ancestry, since he has heard of possible white planter connections. When, in following this biological trail Bob discovers a (black) skeleton in his (English) closet, binarist concepts of race, ancestry, civilised/savage, home and foreign are inverted and thus destabilised and displaced. Moreover, Bob's deep investment in a biological ancestry is rendered almost comically simplistic in the context of the complications of the cultural/representational/biological 'ancestry' of an interpellated colonial subject like Moses. Blood and colour are demonstrated by the novel to be a very small factor in any consideration of self-identity, and Moses rightly dismisses Bob's 'revelation' as the minor matter it clearly is. But in its comedic destabilisation of colonialist stereotypes relative to race-purity, 'motherland', migrancy, exploration and travel, *Moses Migrating* attests to the continuing power of these 'stereotropes ' at the same time as it critiques the simplicity of binarist categorisations in comparison with the complex linguistic and cultural 'ties that bind' the colonial subject.

It is through Moses' carnival costume that Selvon brings together his critique of colonialist stereotropes. Initially Moses does not intend to play mas, but having considered the available avenues for prosecuting his 'civilising mission' he reasons that a carnival costume demonstrating his unshakeable faith that the 'coin of the (English) realm 'is still the 'real McCoy ' is the most fruitful course to pursue.

The representation of Britannia (or the King's or Queen's head) on coins offers an example of a near literal stereotype - one that is also iconic of empire and foreign rule as it operates as everyday 'exchange ' in the lives of colonial subjects. In George Lamming's *In the Castle of My Skin* school children discuss at length the 'technology' by which the King's head is 'impressed' on a coin, inquiring into the processes and power by which the icon is 'fixed' and endlessly circulated as currency. In Moses' decision to dress not just as Britannia but as the representation of Britannia on the English penny Selvon not only demonstrates the historical connection between money and colonialism (and mocks Moses' contemporary civilising mission to support the English pound) but does so in the form of an almost literal stereotype that symbolises basic modes of exchange in a colonial context, one with its foundations in slavery where Africans were literally European exchange/coin. Moreover English Britannia - female symbol of (white) British power - is here represented by a black male Moses.

But Moses is persuaded by Tanty and Doris to involve Jeannie as a white hand-maiden and Bob as the 'slave' who will pull Britannia's chariot. He rationalises these additions as suitable support for the English symbol, but the Carnival judges and audience, far from apprehending the pageant as pro-British and currency supporting, read his representation subversively - as a counter-colonial inversion of the historical hierarchy. His costume also carries a reminder of the ironies of British educational practice where West Indian children were obliged to learn by heart and sing on school parade grounds the anthem 'Rule Britannia, Britannia rule the waves/Britons never never shall be slaves.' Moses' 'obedient' gesture is thus interpreted by his Trinidadian audience as deeply disobedient, and he wins the prize.

But there is a further twist to Moses' Carnival costume and performance. In his masquerade of Britannia, Moses literally represents both sides of the coin (significantly he has to have white English Bob pull his chariot round to demonstrate this to the judges) and in so far as he thus renders a static image (a stereotype) mobile, and provokes the opposite interpretation from that which he intended, his performance is metonymic of Selvon's mobilisation and destabilisation of stereotypes and stereotropes in *Moses Migrating*. Through his novels, Selvon puts both sides of the coin back together, as it were, and sets it spinning.

But it is not just the stereotropes of empire and their colonial and post-colonial repetitions of which Selvon is critical. In *Moses Migrating* be also interrogates counter-colonial strategies which invoke racial, national, or 'nativist' essentialisms - strategies still rooted in the same binary codifications and thus dealing in (neo) stereotypical figurations. So Moses resists the trajectory that seems to be leading him 'home' to (little) Doris, the trajectory of an essentialist return to 'roots', in favour of an ambivalent return, as a 'norphan', to his 'other' 'London' home. There, brandishing his 'holy grail' (the Carnival trophy) as proof of his loyalty to the realm (though it was awarded for his subverting of the historical paradigm) Moses as both traveller and resident, returning child and foreign migrant, waits as the English entry officer goes off to check his passport.

NOTES

1. Peter Nazareth, 'Interview with Sam Selvon', *World Literature Written in English* 18, 2 (1979)), pp.423-424.
2. See for example Kenneth Ramchand, 'Song of Innocence, Song of Experience: Samuel Selvon's *The Lonely Londoners* as a Literary Work', *World Literature Written in English*, 21, 3 (1982) pp.644-654.
3. See for example Edward Baugh, 'Friday in Crusoe City: The Question of Language in Two West Indian Novels of Exile', (*ACLALS* Bulletin, 5th Series, 3 1980) pp1-12. and Helen Tiffin, 'Post Colonial Literatures and Counter-Discourse', (*Kunapipi* 9, 3 1987) pp.17-39.
4. An exception to this is Jeremy Poynting's perspective article 'Samuel Selvon, *Moses Migrating*' in Susheila Nasta ed. *Critical Perspectives on Sam Selvon* (Washington: Three Continents, 1988), pp.260-265.

5. Homi Bhabha, *The Location of Culture* (London: Routledge, 1994), p.67.
6. Thomas B. Macaulay, 'Minute on Indian Education' in *Speeches of Lord Macauley with his Minute on Indian Education* ed. G.M. Young (Oxford: Oxford U.P., 1935).
7. Samuel Selvon, *Moses Ascending* (London: Davis-Poynter.), p.37.
8. *The Housing Lark* (1965) offers an example of the way in which Selvon takes a cliché (chickens coming home to roost) and elaborates it, denaturalising it by giving it historical grounding, and then placing this history in ironic or inverted relation to the present:
'By the time the coach reach Hampton Court you would think the party went out for the day and now coming home to roost in the palace (p.112). The West Indians are indeed the colonial 'chickens coming home to roost', taking possession of their rightful inheritance, that which their education taught was theirs while their skins/bodies/history relegated them to the status of colonised others. The play on poultry/poetry, the echo of the English expression 'chickens coming home to roost' is elaborated over the next five pages. The West Indian visitors/owners imagine Henry VIII himself looking out the window and sizing up his chicks - his women (all envisaged as existing simultaneously) and this 'historical' imaginative flight is followed by: 'And suppose Old Henry was still alive and he look out the window and see all these swarth characters walking about in his gardens!' (p.117-118) - not his 'chicks' now, but the 'chickens come home to roost' the return of a history of exploration, genocide and exploitation that began in the Renaissance period.
9. Samuel Selvon, *Moses Migrating* (London: Longman, 1983), p.61.
10. Ibid., P.10.

LOUIS JAMES

Sam Selvon

The eponymous hero of Sam Selvon's *Moses Ascending* (1975), an east Indian from Trinidad, buys a tenement house in Shepherd's Bush, West London. He also acquires Bob, a white Man Friday 'from somewhere in the Midlands, a willing worker, eager to learn the ways of the Black Man'. Moses tries unsuccessfully to convert Bob from the evils of alcohol. 'I decided to teach him the Bible when I could make the time.' The account of Moses's trials with Bob typifies Selvon's writings, witty, pointed and good-humoured, giving a Caribbean twist to a familiar theme.

Selvon was born in 1923 in South Trinidad, and educated in the semi-rural town of San Fernando. His father, a dry-goods merchant, was a first-generation East Indian immigrant to Trinidad, and his mother was Anglo-Scottish. His education ended with high school - his parents could not afford more - and he showed no ambition to take up a life in one of the professions. It was during long hours as a wireless operator in the Royal Navy in the Second World War that he turned seriously to writing. When demobbed, he became sub-editor of the *Trinidad Guardian Weekly*, one of the few writing outlets on the island.

The post-war years were a time of extraordinary literary activity in the Caribbean, with many who would later gain international reputations exploring their talents. These included George Lamming, Derek Walcott, Kamau (then Edward) Brathwaite. Wilson Harris and V. S. Naipual. Selvon's editorial work helped put him in touch with some of this activity, and his short stories began to appear in *Bim*, a seminal West Indian 'little magazine' and on the BBC.

In 1950 Selvon was one of the wave of Caribbean immigrants coming to England in search of fame and 'streets paved with gold'. He found neither, and there followed a hungry period, living in an immigrant hostel, then in a basement flat in Notting Hill, West London. This was to prove a formative period, turning a writer with yearnings to write romantic accounts of Trinidad (an early influence was Richard Jeffreys), into a sharp observer of the vagaries of immigrant life. In 1952 he published *A Brighter Sun*, and excellent reviews encouraged him to become a full-time writer.

A Brighter Sun is set in Trinidad, and he continued to write well about his home island. But he will be remembered first as the chronicler of black immigrant city life, the subject of *The Lonely Londoners* (1956), its sequels, *Moses Ascending* (1975) and *Moses Migrating* (1983), and a range of brilliant short stories. The best known of these is perhaps 'Brackley and the Bed', a tale which often featured in his public readings. Brackley, an easy-going Tobagan, is pursued to England by the teriffying Teena, who sets about reforming him and his tiny bed-sitting room. Teena takes over Brackley's bed and, reduced to a blanket on the floor, he is driven in desperation for sleep to marry Teena. But after the marriage ceremony Teena breaks into Brackley's fantasies of slumber by announcing she has now invited 'Auntie' to England to live with them. And 'she can sleep with me until we find another place'.

The story can be read at many levels, from the undermining of the sexual stereotypes of the West Indian male, to a parable about the immigrant's lack of roots. But the story's genius lies in its wit, its brilliant timing, and Selvon's miraculous transcription of the Caribbean idiom into written English. He starts not from formal European models, but from the strategies of the Caribbean calypso, the tall story told in rum-shop or on the verandah, and what Selvon himself calls the 'ballad'. His anecdotal style is Trinidadian, yet it remains accessible to readers across the varying creoles of the Caribbean, and, equally, to non-West-Indians.

Selvon's humour at first worked against his critical reputation. Although one of the most widely read and anthologised writers of the Anglophone Caribbean, he was sometimes dismissed as a lightweight entertainer. Yet *The Lonely Londoners* (1956) was a pioneer in its use throughout of Caribbean creole, and his success in using the idiom stimulated the linguistic liberation of Caribbean and other non-British writing from the bonds of 'standard English'. His importance has been increasingly recognised. With Horace Ové he wrote the script for the first British West Indian film, *Pressure* (1975). Despite moving to Calgary, Alberta, in 1978, he received numerous literary honours and awards, including doctorates from the universities of the West Indies and Sussex. He was much sought after on the international conference and lecture circuits.

There was an element of Selvon himself in the Moses of his London books, wandering with the immigrant tribes in the wilderness of Bayswater and Marble Arch. Yet there is also an element of self-parody. Selvon was the most gentle, self effacing of men, hardly a Moses. The pressures of late success would have been hard to cope with, had he not been protected by many friends world-wide. To the end he remained extraordinarily unaffected by fame, a warm and sensitive personality whose art and persona formed a seamless whole. It is fitting that, after a life of exile, he should have come home in the end to Trinidad.

KEN RAMCHAND

The Patient
(for Michael, Leslie and Debbie)

Editor's Note: *This story is based upon the last weeks in the life of Sam*
Selvon who died in a hospital in Trinidad.

The Korean woman what tell Jerry to bring some Frank Sinatra records
for me (I don't know what kiskadee tell she I even listen to Frank Sinatra
record), that same bitch pushing her mouth against my ears as if is a
trumpet, getting on just like that writer feller what look at a big man like
me and tell me he love me.

   She come to announce that they carrying me to Canada in a special
plane: 'Saam, Saam darling, I know you're hearing me, Saam, I have
something to tell you but you mustn't get angry you hearing me? I want
you to be a good boy?'

   What the ass is this? Who have more causes to be obedient more than
me? Who could want this sickness to pass more than me?

   Afterwards, the boy in whose veins the poem sang left his companions sitting
on the steps of the railway station and wandered off for more poetry, discovering
it in the sleeping village and the flower-strewn lane by the cemetery, and in the
flowers which appeared to explode into efflorescence. A clear stream ran through
the village. Engraved on a clock high on the steeple of an old church were the
words. 'Grow old along with me, the best is yet to be.'

   It surprise everybody how meek I get in the hospital. I abide by all the
rules, and I follow every instruction. Keep my mouth quiet when I know
the care is not intensive care. Kick up no fuss when a female patient
whose head can't be right, leave her own bed and come to lay down in
mine, and nearly tangle on all them wires and hoses that tying me
down. Make no complaint when a nurse get confuse and try to give me a
tablet and I know, from the colour, that is a tablet the doctor who come
this morning decide he not giving me again.

   It have no dignity in it this helplessness. I keep still while they do all
the shit that they have to do for me. I don't flinch when they invent some
new procedure, some new pain that they have to inflict. I make no
complaints. Sometimes I think I will go mad on this hopeless, heartless
mount, but I refuse. If it is time they want to clear up what has to clear
up, is all right, I am fighting. I am giving them time.

   Blinding shocking sensations crossed crisscross in his brain as the little men began their macabre work. He longed for death as the blunt pegs thudded against and split open the skin of his forehead, then met unresisting bone. Armies marched in his brain, all the drums in the world boomed, cymbal clashed, the Kalteur Falls roared. And yet, with a grimness impossible to conceive he clung tenaciously to reason, preferring to die than be driven into the looming limbo of the ring of deep purple, and everytime he thought that he could bear it no more, some itch of life stirred and came forward.

Haul all you ass, little men.

The first time the hospital send me home was a happy time. I remind the short bitch how he make me go outside in the Colgate snow everytime I want to light up and smoke. Then I tell him not to worry it wouldn't happen again, I finish with that, boy. If they are looking for a famous face to advertise how smoking is bad, and how liquor will lick you up before your time, they don't have to look far, they could come and take out my photo any day.

Three times they let me out, and is three times I had was to go back. The Black Englishwoman tell Junior they didn't really have to admit me again, but they like to be absolutely sure.

When they let me go for the third time, they still telling me I can't leave right away. They playing up in they ass. I didn't want to wait to ten days again just for them to make sure I could go by myself. But seven days pass and I am feeling so nice, I start to believe I will travel on Sunday for sure. I drink a cold Carib because the doctors say one drink a day is good medicine for the heart. I almost feel I could take a smoke. The temptation strong. But not me, boy. A year or two from now when I forget the terror I pass through. I have a feeling the battle will be hard. But not now. Not so soon.

But Friday morning it is fever and pain, and when Junior come for us to drink some coffee before the Test match start, I don't have the pride to put on appearance to fool no man. I have to hold on to the walking stick with two hands, bend my head over; and let my belly squeeze in order to breathe. The Black English doctor ask me some fucking questions she shouldn't be asking a man of my age, and shouldn't be asking after I in the hospital so long. I am glad Junior didn't hear because he would have make some joke about how I am just like Syl and I can't even recognise a drawing of the thing, and how it is so long since I bounce up one he could bet I wouldn't know the difference between a picture of it and a dry coconut.

I feel as if I am dying this time. As if something clog and the air reach a wall at the top of my nose, and when I pull with my mouth, air jamming again at the back of my throat. I can't believe it. These mother asses don't know what is wrong with me. They are putting me under observation which mean I have to lie down, and they are going to wait and see.

For three days nobody observe that I am fighting for air. On Sunday I prop up in the bed struggling as usual to breathe, and the nurse get up

and leave saying your friend come. The next thing I know is like Junior
gone crazy in the place. I hear him telling somebody he don't care one
fuck, he is a fucking doctor too, and he know that fucking man stifling,
and they better find some way of giving him some fucking oxygen before
he dead. The fucking man he talking about is me. If I wasn't frighten
before, I frighten no arse now.

By Sunday night they have me on something called a life-support
system. They tell everybody they ventilating me. Ventilating. After weeks
and weeks of 'Nothing ain't wrong is only the medication to adjust', they
change they mind and decide the problem is the lungs. The Black
woman with the English accent say in she funny voice that the lungs full
of Gunk. If is scrabble she playing, I could think of plenty other four
letter words.

Weeks now of the needle's prick, of black and blue and red, of the flesh
bruised and dug up and plastered over, of tubes in my mouth, in my
nose, in my throat, and in openings drilled in chest, in neck, in arm, in
leg. I studying how I am paying all this money and they are tearing me
up, and just so I start to remember the song they teach you to sing when
you small and stupid in school. *Je te plumerai la tete. Et le nez. Et le dos. Oh
Oh.* They suctioning through my mouth, they suctioning through my
nose, and the same Korean woman wants to make a by-pass and suction
through an opening she will cut in my chest.

Every day is a different doctor, everyday is a different story. Each new
doctor have his favourite medicine he itching to try. You remember 'goes
in goes out' where who get the ball, bowl and whoever knock down the
wicket, bat? It is goes in goes out they playing on my head, and every
man Ambrose pelting ball at my arse. If things wasn't so serious in truth,
I could raise a laugh and make a ballad out of these hospital blues.

I am a man of words and I could tell you, the metaphors and similies
these doctors using would put Lamming and Naipaul to shame. Some of
them playing police and thief, some of them fighting guerrilla war. Hear
them. They can't make a positive i.d. but they have some clues. They
eliminate some suspects, and they closing in on the elusive bacteria.
Getting on as if they want to hold press conference to announce they
have a strong lead, but time after time, the lead led to nothing in the end.
The pot-belly man say he can't be sure if the one they pin-point is the
culprit for true, or just an innocent bystander. Assness.

I should be glad they put me in a coma to keep me alive, but this is not
the way I want to live. Day in day out, I can't talk, I can't eat, I can't
drink, I can't pee, I can't shit. Most of the time, the shapes and colours
that cross my eyes are shadows I can't name. If I imagine hard, some of
the sounds I hear turn into words. I know in my heart of hearts that I am
going. The day Jerry and Junior look at me and say I had lovely skin and
now they looking at dead man's flesh, water tried to come to my eyes: I
am angry that it is ending like this, but I try to tell myself there is always

an ending. I have always known.

There is a joy in living because you know you are going to die, and nothing can affect that one way or another. But what I am deeply afraid of is that when the final call comes, I may break down and become a jibbering piece of frightened humanity.

But when the *bodi* vine finish bearing aint it does dead? Everything does dead when it finish the work it have to do. Still for all that I am glad this dying is slow. Have I finished my work? This absorbing silence is an infinite space, and I have drifted in it towards truths that give fight to words. The work I have done. The work I did not do.

There is greatness in the written word, and when men die what they have said will live and sing for other hearts.

Aspirations of the artist as a young man. Sunlight. Thunder. Islands. Worlds. Pinpricks on an unmarked sky. Little drops of water. Little lights.

I lie and think of those I love and those who love me, I have never been this close to the woman since those windy days, and I cannot even raise a finger to let her know.

My girl, she is beautiful to look at. I have seen her in sunlight and in moonlight, and her face carves an exquisite shape in darkness. These things we talk, I burst out, why musn't I say them? If I love you, why shouldn't I tell you so? I love London she said.

All the words I have gathered to say to her at last. I had gathered many times before, and always when I reached to the edge of utterance, something would happen to make me hold back, as if saying the truth would be too complete a surrender, as if I must wait and let her be the one to break the silence, as if the heart that sang in the darkness of the lonely city could not free itself from its own choking. 'What's the Use', as if love's innocent life-line snaps as soon as it starts to find out about life.

I have not said it, but she knows it now.

Eh, eh. All of a sudden the great hospital changing their tune. The long 'Je te plumerai' is over. They have plumerai'd me into silence, immobility and the odour of death. *They have done all they can. They cannot find the bacteria. If I improve, it will not be because of anything they do. The best course now is to send me abroad. It might be a virus and the colder countries have more experience with viruses.*

I smile to myself, and Junior is looking at me as if he is expecting me to say 'What fuckery'. I do not know what a nancy story they spin for the insurance company to spend all that money and send flying ambulance for me.

My wife, she loves me, and she wants me to come home. Oh, but when I think. Still, if this journey and this peace between the woman and me can bring some healing, and make me at last the father and family man I have been in my secret heart, my spirit shall return to day and life like a backward sunset.

My private jet is waiting. But I know what the native legend says.

Whether I go or whether I stay is not for me to decide. I don't know what will happen when they move me from this bed. I don't know what will happen on the road to the airport. I can't tell what will happen when they try to load me onto the aeroplane.

The land knows, I have always trusted the land. Whatever it decides will bring me peace.

Leaving the island this time; there was a great deal of anguish because so much had been left unsaid and undone...let cockcrow and early bird whistle make the decision for me: let the green mountain spin a coin in the first rays of the sun, and when it was light enough I'd enlist the crystals of dew and the gossamer strands that spiders had miraculously spun in space, and pass the buck to them too.

I have always loved the land (even more than the people) and it was not too much to ask. Whatever the land gave I took without question, and it had sent me away and it had brought me back, and it had a certain responsibility which it respected.

CECIL GRAY

Your Island, Your World
(In memory Sam Selvon)

With that loping stoop
you bore down on me like
an eagle (as I imagined one)
and asked me to write
someting for the Sunday
Guardian magazine you
put out. Me, who thought
writers lived on Parnassus
(a mountain I'd heard of).

But youth is impetuous.
I went home and scribbled
an implausible story that
you printed. (I still have
the page I clipped out.)
And some nights I walked
the two blocks between
our homes and tried
to tap inside your words
the vein feeding your pulse.

You seemed to a blind
fumbler a mystic of sorts,
one mad enough to think
about leaving the island
to write. Openmouthed
I watched you depart.

Then you took the small
language used by the island
for picong and calypsoes
and stretched its vowels
across the mouth of the world.
Placed us, as raw as uncured
rum, with every sweet nuance

we used for survival, in pubs
and underground stations
of London. Took Brackley
and Moses out of Rose Hill
and gave them a stature
Micawber once had
in the classrooms that
censored the tongue
our thoughts found ease in.

Yet at home some giggled,
still ashamed. Wondered
how Englishmen took it,
your bold spurning of what
the schools still frowned at.
You were half-disowned.
Then, as usual, when foreign
approval tendered your fame,
when laughter they heard
came from white far-away
continents it was OK
to lay claim to your name.

That time in Croydon
we spoke long about ways
sunlight shone in your pages.
The bitter cane had already given
its liquor to all lonely
Londoners, squeezed from
the Caroni plains, and
girls in that city wanted
to clip like Delilah
your fast-greying mane.
But you had eaten the
bone-filled cascadura,
so again and again you
returned to the thunder
you heard in your heart,
needing the heckles of
Gallows, of Bat.

Rest now. Your pen has
done all of its work. Tiger
lives, Urmilla stoops at a
standpipe washing away

the last traces of race
you sent to her to get rid of.
Sir Galahad has touched
your shoulder with time's
irrevocable knighthood.
I never delivered the tales
of the place you expected,
save a few. See my wreath
like an O in my sorrow.

But then I knew every
square mile gave you its
story, each dustpile its gold.
All of it was your island,
all of it your world.

NOTES ON CONTRIBUTORS

AUSTIN CLARKE grew up in Barbados and has published several novels about immigrant life in Canada where he now lives.

REED DASENBROCK recently edited a collection of interviews with post-colonial writers.

DAVID DABYDEEN is a novelist and poet. He teaches at the University of Warwick.

CECIL GRAY is a poet based in Trinidad.

WILSON HARRIS is a well-known Guyanese writer and critic who now lives and works in London.

JESSICA HUNTLEY is one of the founders of Bogle L'Ouverture publishers.

LOUIS JAMES teaches English at the University of Kent.

FEROZA JUSSAWALLA recently edited a collection of interviews with post-colonial writers.

ISMITH KHAN is an East Indian novelist from Trinidad, who grew up with Sam Selvon. He now lives in New York.

SUSHEILA NASTA is editor of *Wasafiri* and teaches at the University of London, Queen Mary & Westfield College. She is author of *Critical Perspectives on Sam Selvon*.

GRACE ECHE OKEREKE teaches at the University of Calabar, Nigeria.

KEN RAMCHAND teaches at the University of the West Indies in Trinidad. He is working on a biography of Sam Selvon and edited *Foreday Morning : Selected Prose (1946-88)* by Sam Selvon.

VICTOR RAMRAJ teaches at the University of Calgary and is editor of *Ariel*.

ROYDON SALICK teaches at the University of the West Indies. He is writing a book on Sam Selvon.

HENRY SWANZY was one of the early producers of *Caribbean Voices*, the programme which did so much to support writers such as V S Naipaul, Sam Selvon, Andrew Salkey, George Lamming and many others in the 1950s.

HELEN TIFFIN teaches at the University of Queensland. She has written widely in the area of post-colonial literature, and has co-edited *The Empire Writes Back* and *Decolonising Fictions*.

ANNA RUTHERFORD teaches at the University of Aarhus. She is editor of *Kunapipi* and director of Dangaroo Press.

ANNE WALMSLEY is a freelance writer, critic and editor.